FRENCH LEAVES

Letters from the Languedoc

Published by

ROMARIN
Flat 1, 66 Hencroft St South,
SLOUGH
SL1 1RE
United Kingdom
(+44) (0)1753 674557
www.romarin.net

ISBN: 0-9543350-0-7

(First published 2001 by Gopher Publishers UK. ISBN: 90-5179-001-5. This
edition, with minor amendments, published by Romarin 2002)

FRENCH LEAVES

Letters from the Languedoc

Christopher Campbell-Howes

Christopher Campbell-Howes

Line drawings by Andrew Campbell-Howes

ROMARIN
Slough
United Kingdom

for Fiona and Andrew

with love

Author's Note

In 1991 I left Morayshire, in Scotland, where I had been teaching for many years, and set up house in the south of France, in the beautiful and very diverse region called the Languedoc, the curve of Mediterranean littoral and its often mountainous hinterland which stretches from the foothills of the Pyrenees to the river Rhone and the borders of Provence.

A year or two into this new experience Stephen Young, then Editor of *The Northern Scot,* a fine regional newspaper based in Elgin, asked me to contribute a fortnightly article about life in the Languedoc. The pieces that make up this book are a distillation from the 170-odd articles that winged their way every other weekend from my desk to his.

Several house-moves, a personal reorientation and the lack of chronological order may account for some of the unexplained inconsistencies, false trails and disappearances without trace in what follows. You may not notice any. *Tant mieux,* as they say here. So much the better.

Olargues, 2002

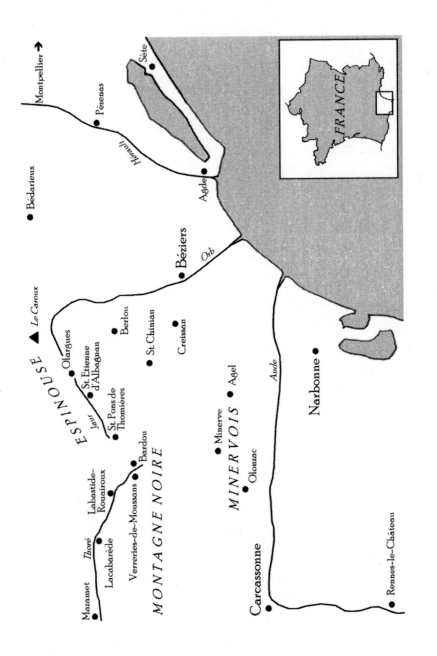

Montpellier →

Sète

Pézenas

Hérault

Agde

FRANCE

Bédarieux

Béziers

Orb

▲ _Le Caroux_

ESPINOUSE

Olargues

St. Etienne
d'Albagnan

Berlou

St. Chinian

Creissan

Jaur

St. Pons de
Thomières

MINERVOIS

Agel

Aude

Narbonne

Minerve

Bardou

MONTAGNE NOIRE

Olonzac

Labastide–
Rouairoux

Verreries-de-Moussans

Thoré

Mazamet

Lacabarède

Carcassonne

Rennes-le-Château

7

BARDOU

Nous Voici!

'How brave you are!' people said, when they heard we were leaving to set up home in France. 'We're so envious!'

Brave? To give up a secure and well-paid job (well, paid, anyway), a comfortable house with a large garden and wide views over a beautiful stretch of Scottish countryside and to cast off into the unknown with no visible means of support? To abandon as flourishing a musical life as any hack musician has a right to expect?

Reckless, maybe; but it seemed such a simple and attractive formula, to sell up in Scotland and buy in France. It was an idea that had germinated slowly, starting as a mere wouldn't-it-be-wonderful-if, swelling irresistibly to a what-are-we-waiting-for kind of impatience. The right moment seemed to have come when interest rates grew engagingly high: French property prices were a fraction of their UK counterparts, so the surplus from the sale ought to provide a modest income for a year or two. At last there would be freedom, and time, to write the novels which had been bubbling away for years, without having to get up at dawn every morning to pen a few crabbed words before donning the suit and the persona of a primary school head teacher.

All France was our oyster, but we deliberately chose the Languedoc. It seemed pointless to go all that way without finding somewhere to settle in the southern sun. There were other reasons: the Languedoc was undiscovered and undeveloped. Nobody that we knew of wrote seductive books about it. It seldom appeared in the overseas property sections of *The Scotsman* or *The Sunday Times*, so it was a fairly safe bet that it wasn't knee-deep in compatriots urging us to join bridge clubs or cricket teams, as reputedly happened in more popular areas like the Dordogne. Fewer foreign incomers meant less likelihood of inflated house prices. Everything pointed to the deep South.

We were surprised by what we found. It's a region of extraordinary beauty and unexpected diversity. The *massif central*, the great granite central upland of France, stops short of the Mediterranean basin in a series of rocky escarpments and foothills, dividing the Languedoc into *haut* and *bas*, high and low. The Bas Languedoc is mainly coastal plain, supporting the world's largest concentration of vineyards, interspersed with peach orchards, olive groves and fruit and vegetable plantations, strawberries, melons, courgettes and aubergines. The roads are straight and the villages, each with their nucleus of ancient, sun-bleached, cheek-by-jowl houses, are growing outwards fast with measles-like rashes of two-up, two-down – or the French equivalent – villas housing the bourgeois overspill from Béziers and the region's administrative centre, Montpellier. Here and there along the endless sands of the coastline there are still gaps in the mushrooming beach complexes where shore and saltmarsh show little sign of the developer's hand, but they're becoming fewer and farther between.

The Haut Languedoc is quite different. Most of it lies at over 900 metres. It's a country of sparsely populated rolling uplands, cattle pastures, pine forests, granite villages with roofs of slate or *lauzes*, stone slabs, with wide overhangs to keep the snow off the woodpile or the threshold; or gorge-slashed limestone *plateaux* where thin-fleeced, threadbare sheep roam, kept for the milk that ancient skills and modern machinery turn into Roquefort and Bleu des Causses, twin kings of blue cheese.

But in between Haut and Bas lies a band of country unlike anywhere else in France. Most of the weather comes in from the west, from the Atlantic, carrying the frequent rains that make the northern and western slopes so green and densely forested. This is the country where the winter *tramontane*, the north wind, and the *albigeois*, the west wind blowing in from the direction of Albi, can spend days on end hurling wraiths and skeins of mist and cloud up the valleys. They rattle spatters of rain against the shutters and send sprays down the chimney to hiss among the logs of beech and ash on the hearth. It is weather to make you draw closer to the fire, or, if you have to go out, clutch your collar closer about your throat, keep your head down and long for summer.

And this is the country we settled in, to start with, on the wrong side of the Atlantic-Mediterranean watershed. We should have been sharper. Lush pastures, thick broadleaved forests and dense greenery should have spelt out R-A-I-N. We should have guessed what the robust local patois nickname for the area, *Lou Pissadou*, actually implied. Even in the height of summer, when we did our exploring, the clues were there. There's none so blind as those that will not see.

A little farther, a few kilometres to the east and south, everything changes. The hills and valleys lie in the rain shadow and the countryside becomes truly Mediterranean. On the south-facing slopes the Languedoc's best grapes ripen for harvest in September: wines from Faugères, St Chinian and the Minervois travel all over the world. Rock-perched villages alternate with hamlets clinging to the parent rock like hibernating snails, the land is terraced with ancient drystone walls, sweet chestnut woods border modest family vineyards, the yellow of the mimosa gives way to the pink of almond, then to the white of cherry blossom in early spring. The hills are covered in *chêne vert*, a dense, slow-growing evergreen oak, and the tops are scented with the wild thyme, rosemary and juniper of the scrub known as the *garrigue*. Here crickets sing from dawn to dusk, buzzards and eagles ride the thermals, dogs bark at their echos across the valley, distant bells ring hours which pass less hurriedly than anywhere else in the known world.

Maybe we should have recognised the finger of providence pointing us in this direction when we first tried to buy a house in *Lou Pissadou*. During an exploratory sortie one summer, when sunshine to die for gave no inkling of the dreichness of the winters, we discovered in a remote and densely wooded valley what seemed to be half a village for sale: houses, garages, stabling and outbuildings, one with a bread oven, a jumble of dusty and decrepit property, deep-littered with the junk of ages. The owner, a Monsieur Vidal, had long since moved away, leaving the outside fabric in the care of lizards and the inside to warring clans of *loirs*, a sort of destructive domestic squirrel. There was land, too: a vegetable garden, acres of dark pinewood running no one knew how far up the hill behind the village, other plots of bramble-smothered land we never identified. £11,000. Mesmerised by the sense of adventure and the silly prices, and probably by a touch of the sun too, we jumped at it, signed along several dotted lines and went home to Scotland in high spirits.

Autumn turned to winter without any news from France. Questioned in halting French over the telephone, the estate agent prevaricated and eventually admitted that there was a problem. M. Vidal had acted in good faith, but the genealogical search that goes with house purchase had rattled a few skeletons in somebody's cupboard: M. Vidal did indeed own the property, but so did three half-sisters in Italy, whose existence was news to him. The sisters were delighted, as well they might be; it isn't every day you discover that you own an interesting property in the south of France, let alone the half-brother that goes with it. No, they said, they didn't want to sell, they wanted to enjoy it.

So we smiled ruefully and started again, in the same area, and this time we ended up with a 200-year-old *bergerie* with a small garden in the hamlet of Bardou, where the dogs outnumbered the inhabitants, where the arrival of a family from Scotland set them barking as they'd never barked before: Bardou, a hamlet of 11 stone-built, ochre-tiled houses tucked away in a quiet fold of the last hills before the Mediterranean. Whatever the French is for Sleepy Hollow, this was it. The estate agent didn't say that in winter this was one of the wettest places in Europe.

A *bergerie*? They're quite common here: a barn or steading for wintering sheep or goats, a three-storey building in stone, with the ground floor for the beasts, middle floor, maybe with some rudimentary accommodation for the shepherd or goatherd, for storing hay and the top floor, underneath the eaves, for pigeons. The previous owners had converted it into a no-frills summer weekend house, putting in a window here and a door there, building out a *terrasse* or deck looking down the valley, adding a flight of stairs to the mezzanine that was to become our library, installing one of those standing-only loos *à la turque* which are always mystifying to find among as comfort-loving a people as the French. But they hadn't done much, bècause it was barely needed in summer, to adapt to everyday use the huge 2-metre wide fireplace with a chimney breast sweeping up to lose itself among the roof timbers of gnarled chestnut trunks.

The fireplace gave trouble from the start. For all its majestic size, from the first ceremonial match it smoked abominably. Heaping wood on to create a roaring inferno sucked icy draughts from every crevice and chink, every ill-fitting window frame, every *loir*-hole in the eaves. The hotter the fire, the colder the house became. We hung a curtain from the mantelpiece, the time-honoured Languedoc smoke reduction method. But to no purpose: how could we entertain the neighbours and introduce ourselves in a kiln, a smoke-house?

Eventually the problem was solved by raising both the chimney and the hearth and by laying the fire in a basket grate. Difficulties with the draught were never entirely overcome. To get the fire to burn brightly the back door had to be left ajar. However, by the time the first guest's tap on the door came, on Christmas Eve, the house was bright, warm and you could see from one end of the room to the other.

They all came, probably as much out of curiosity as anything. Thérèse, the *doyenne* of the village, sharp and spry still in her 80s; Emilie, an elderly lady whose gales of laughter matched her colossal girth; her taciturn son Justin, a forestry and public works contractor and Conso, whom he was proud to introduce as his *concubine*; Pierrot, who honoured us by actually taking his hat off in the house; Jean-Claude, a doctor from Narbonne, and his wife Marie-Jo, who had a weekend and holiday house in the village, like his namesake, the other Jean-Claude, a carpenter from near Béziers, and his wife Josie. With Francis, a far-left and soon-to-retire railwayman and his wife Ginou, a hairdresser, who dressed all the hairs of Bardou for nothing as a sort of community rent for the enjoyment she got out of their tiny slice of a weekend cottage, the entire population of Bardou, or all that were there that Christmas Eve, found itself in our sitting room. We fed them on mince pies, a novelty to them, and good red wine. They showed a talent for enjoying themselves which could probably be appreciated down the valley in the next village, Les Verreries de Moussans.

When they left, some to attend Midnight Mass, some to prepare their *réveillon*, their watchnight meal, some to see Christmas in in the Bar du Centre down the valley in Labastide, it had stopped raining. A good augury, we felt. We'd arrived.

Bon Appetit!

Hungry? We were then and I am again, just writing about it: the communal meal, highlight of the social year in Bardou. That we are there at all is a measure of the welcome *les Bardousiens* have shown us.

We sit down to table at about 9.15, under a velvet summer evening sky hung with a crisp new moon and a thousand stars, shining more brilliantly as the twilight deepens, the warm night air richly scented with mouth-watering wafts of good things cooking. All the village is there, and every sister, cousin and aunt that can be gathered in: Emilie, often calling for her little dog Pompon and shaking with laughter when told he is lying quietly at her feet, hidden from view by her majestic bust; Thérèse, her hair newly done by Ginou for the occasion, the gravel-voiced Francis, and so on down the line of rickety trestle tables and borrowed plastic garden furniture to Pierrot at the end, complete as always with black leather trilby hat and shirt open almost to the waist. Pierrot is starting to tell a complicated joke about a sausage left behind on the moon by Neil Armstrong and found by the angels.

Forty-eight places have been set, each marked by an upturned plate with the occupant's name written on it. I find myself next to Jean-Claude, the doctor who comes up most summer weekends to escape the torrid heat of Narbonne, a fascinating Roman town 50 kilometres away to the south.

Jean-Claude and I agree what a pleasure it is to eat out of doors in the evening, a pleasure rare indeed in Scotland. He is surprised, even a little disappointed, to learn that the practice of a small community taking an occasional meal together hardly exists north of the English Channel. I'm spared having to describe Jubilee street parties or Burns Suppers by a sudden hush in the conversation and the arrival of the first course, a wicker basket of *crudités*.

There are beautifully-flavoured tomatoes the size of apples, stalks of crisp celery, cucumbers, lettuce, peppers and sprigs of raw crunchy cauliflower, to be eaten with *tapenade* (crushed and seasoned black olives) or with a meltingly delicious anchovy sauce, both of which our neighbour Josie has made. There are *baguettes* of crusty bread to mop the last smears of sauce and to wipe your knife and fork on, because they'll be needed for the other courses. We drink water, freshly drawn from the spring just down the lane.

Next, a dish of *charcuterie*, cured and smoked meats, slices of sausage seasoned with herbs and peppers, a delectable mousse of duck. Mmm, delicious. Wine is served, a local *vin du pays* from unlabelled bottles. Meanwhile, Pierrot's angels have taken their moon-booty for identification to St Peter, who is quite baffled by what it can be. So are we, but knowing Pierrot I suspect the ending will be robust, if not earthy.

A cheer goes up for the next course, a *daube* of beef which has been simmering nearby in a huge cauldron, waiting for this moment, the climax of the meal. Reverently marinaded and seethed in a rich broth of white wine, herbs and Armagnac, it is a treat for the gods, a privilege to eat, from the first succulent forkful to the last bread-soaked sippet of rich gravy. Josie assures us that the beef is the best in the world, from the bulls of the Camargue.

At the end Jean-Claude calls for silence, just at the point in Pierrot's joke where the angels take their find to the Virgin Mary to see if she knows what it is. We're left hanging while Jean-Claude proposes a toast to the women who have done us so well: Josie, Marie-Jo and Conso (short for Consolation; maybe one day we'll get to know her well enough to ask how she got her name) who have done all the cooking.

And still the good things come: a change of wine, from the unlabelled *vin du pays* to a vintage Minervois, from our local vineyards a few kilometres to the south, chosen especially to accompany the cheese. Fresh fruit, then a chocolate mousse, dark and bittersweet, served with champagne, and finally coffee as the church clock down in the valley strikes midnight. We have been almost three hours at table.

We are wilting by this time, like the village dogs, asleep at their owners' feet, and we begin to make our farewells, a handshake for those we don't know well and *la bise* (the kiss on each cheek) for those we do.

And Pierrot's joke? H'm. As suspected, it turns out to be more than robust. *Risqué*, not to say *coquin*. And quite unrepeatable.

Not like the Bardou village meal. They can repeat it any time. We'll be there.

Escargots? Non, Merci

We drove back to Bardou late one evening just as a summer thunderstorm was abating, leaving behind it a cool night deliciously freshened by the rain. To our surprise, in our yellow headlights we discovered a curious figure lurking by our house, picking things off a rain-washed drystone wall by torchlight and putting them into a plastic bag.

It turned out to be our neighbour Paulette, a pleasant and sophisticated lady, short, slim and dark, who always takes her glasses off for *la bise* to avoid poking you in the eye with the frame. Paulette spends several summer weeks in Bardou, and odd weekends at other seasons too. Her husband Jacques is a banker, a senior official with the Crédit Lyonnais. We don't see very much of them: they spend most of their time in Marseilles. They own two houses in the village, one for themselves and the other for occasional use by their grown-up children. The Jacques-Paulette clan numbers about 12, and the Bardou population doubles when they are all there.

Paulette was collecting snails, drawn out from their hiding places by the damp night air. Her bag was almost full. Most seemed to have come from the wall of our house, which runs along the lane at one point. She must have found at least a hundred, some perhaps technically ours, although I'm by no means certain of the French law governing ownership of snails. In any case she was welcome to them.

No need to ask what she was collecting them for.

She wasn't in the least put out at being discovered. While the thunder rumbled away in the distance, she chattered on merrily, with all the enthusiasm of one who has unexpectedly been presented with a free meal, about which were the tastiest and how she was going to cook them. Did we like them? She liked them best piping hot, with a dressing of melted butter, garlic and parsley. Some people preferred them *à la provençale*, with a dressing of olive oil, tomato and, of course, the indispensable garlic. Which did we prefer? How did we eat them *chez nous*, in Scotland?

Cowards that we are, we didn't tell her that most Scots would rather have their teeth pulled than look hungrily at a snail. Instead we took the soft option and said well, yes, we do have snails in Scotland, but little ones, much too fiddly to eat, not at all the edible kind. Paulette was disappointed that Scotland should be deprived of such a delicacy. She was convinced that there was a solution: it was just a matter of a little determination. Where there was a will there was a way. Couldn't we import them? Even the French had to import them nowadays. Such a shame. There was good money to be made in snail farming. She'd heard of an Englishman who'd started a snail farm over in the Gard, near Nîmes. Nowadays, the best *escargots* came from Germany. Frozen, of course. You could buy them anywhere.

Paulette offered us some of hers. We refused politely, finally admitting that snails were not a Scottish taste and that we really didn't care at all for the idea of eating them. Paulette was sympathetic. Each to his own, after all; it was only natural that there should be differences in national tastes. She herself had once tried to eat turnip, but had found it impossibly revolting.

It started to rain again, so we said goodnight and went in, narrowly avoiding crushing several portions of Paulette's supper gliding happily about the damp stone steps up to our front door. We left Paulette to continue her snail hunt under her yellow umbrella. We could still see her torch ranging about half an hour later. There were snails everywhere. Few can have escaped.

In fact, we had eaten snails once before, more in a spirit of enquiry than for any other reason, in a restaurant which some friends used to run near Versailles. They were served, as they usually are, by the dozen, in tiny cups so hot that they give you a pair of little tongs to hold the cup with while you winkle the contents out with a special fork. They were quite tasty, certainly, with a texture something like kidney, not in the least rubbery, but a lifetime's prejudices are hard to overcome and I wouldn't feel aggrieved if I never ate another.

Not so Paulette and Jacques, eagerly looking forward to the next thunderstorm, as they said in the morning. *Chacun à son goût*, after all.

A-Hunting We Will Go

Bardou is such a sleepy hamlet that you can sense when something out of the ordinary has happened; there's a tension, a sharp chemistry waiting for anyone's sixth sense to pick up. When we woke up one Sunday we were uneasily aware that something untoward had happened, and as soon as we opened the front door we found the place convulsed with the previous night's doings.

Josie, a superb cook, one of the three village ladies responsible for the communal meal a few weeks earlier, up for the weekend with her husband Jean-Claude the carpenter, was agog to tell us. Dressed in combat gear, trousers and tunic camouflaged in greens and browns, with thick-soled ammunition boots to match, she could have stepped out of the set of M*A*S*H in order to slip home to take the washing in - a fancy not too far from the truth, because when we opened our door she was taking her 2-year-old grand-daughter Jessica round the corner to be looked after by Conso while she herself joined *la chasse*.

Battledress? Josie is a huntress, one of the very few women to have penetrated the most macho of male preserves here; *la chasse*, the hunt, sometimes - very engagingly - called *la Diane* after the Roman goddess of hunting. Most weekends she dons the hunting gear, straps on her cartridge belt, slings her 12-bore over her shoulder and strides out with Jean-Claude, their hunting dog Dick (pronounced 'Deek'), their friend Pierrot and the other 15-odd local *chasseurs*. Until, of course, she has to slip home to prepare the midday meal or to settle little Jessica for her afternoon sleep.

The news Josie told us was indeed stunning. During the night *un sanglier*, a wild boar, had broken into Pierrot's garden - not difficult, because there's no fence - and had ravaged every living plant, his tomatoes, his courgettes, his potatoes. It had rolled on his gladioli and flattened his chrysanthemums, and as for his maize, hardly a corncob remained. *La catastrophe*, a complete devastation. The Year The Wild Boar Wrecked Pierrot's Garden will stand out in the slow advance of village history, a beacon of reference for other less turbulent years.

Thérèse joined us, anxious to keep the pot boiling. In 84 years in the village she'd never known anything like it. What was more, she knew where the beast had holed up. He was in the thickets down by the stream, slaking his thirst after such a feast of maize . . . but she was just an old woman, nobody took any notice of what she said.

Just then the hunt arrived, Pierrot, Jean-Claude and Deek among them, snaking down into the village in a tatterdemalion procession of cars and vans, battered and filthy from numberless hunting trips. The first car, towing a home-made trailer once the back end of a yellow Renault 4, and full of barking dogs heaving and jostling to get a better view from the window, stopped by Pierrot's garden, and the rest drew up behind. *Les chasseurs* assembled and began to beat through the boar-ravaged waste, guns at the ready. We had seats in the dress circle, not that the spectacle promised to be a very pretty one.

'*Ils sont fous, ces types-là,*' Thérèse said, without any malice. 'They're daft, those fellows. Of course they won't find him there. He was away hours ago, before dawn.' It was now 9 am, and it seemed unlikely that any *sanglier*, however bloated with maize and tomatoes, would hang about in a empty larder. Not surprisingly the search of Pierrot's garden, hardly bigger than a bowling green, yielded nothing, and presently the cavalcade moved on, a-howl with barking dogs, down the lane to Les Verreries de Moussans.

Pierrot, with a wrecked garden and no culprit, hadn't much to say, simply a stunned '*Eh bé pauvre, pardi, ma foi,*' which the most seasoned translator would have trouble rendering into English, though in Scotland you might get away with some tangled string of interjections like *losh be here, michty aye, ken.* But time would tell. He'd get his maize back, even if they had been metabolised into *sanglier* chops. The vandal couldn't bear a charmed life for ever. His greed would give him away, *ma foi.* Oh! that it might be before hunting season finished in January!

Nobody except us, it seemed, spared a thought for the *sanglier*, but that's just our soft northern attitude to wild animals, which clashes head on with the more robust, pragmatic French ideas. If it's edible, hunt it and eat it. Not so much for the sport, because there can't be much fun in standing alone on a winter's afternoon in your appointed place with only a damp Gauloise for company, waiting for the dogs to flush out a wild boar, deer or mountain goat; more for an almost tribal sense of community and mutual dependance in the sharing out of the carcase. Especially if someone like Josie has already slipped home to light the oven.

Thérèse was right, of course. The Thérèses of this world always are. The stream chatters and tumbles its way from Bardou to Les Verreries de Moussans, a kilometre downstream, where a patchwork of villagers' maize-rich gardens lies beside the water.

Sure enough, early the next morning, just after his father, a butcher, had gone to work, 13-year-old Sébastian Barthès saw from his bedroom window a heaving commotion in a nearby stand of maize, the stalks shaking violently. The news of *la catastrophe* in Pierrot's garden had travelled much faster than *la chasse* had reacted, and Sébastian had his suspicions. He crept downstairs to his father's gun-rack.

One barrel was enough for the *coup de grâce*, and never were M. Barthès' professional skills put to better use than when he returned at lunchtime to find the village seething with excitement, Sébastian the Boy Hero wallowing in popular acclaim and a hefty carcase slumped in the *lavoir*, the public wash-house. The Barthès household enjoyed the prime cuts, and Pierrot had the meagre satisfaction of a few chops and the promise of some *pâté*.

Nobody asked if it was the same *sanglier*, whether it was the hardened garden-wrecking sinner or a saintly innocent, blamelessly enjoying a good scratch when Sébastian lifted the fatal gun-sight. What did it matter? It was a free meal. Perhaps not for Pierrot, but for everyone else, including Thérèse, who purred with self-satisfaction, although she is too nice a person to go about saying 'I told you so'. When we called on her a few days later she was making her share into a *daube* over an open fire of evergreen oak. It was fascinating to watch; we seemed to have penetrated to the very heart of French country cooking.

Thérèse had stood an iron *trépied*, a trivet or tripod, in the fire, supporting a panful of sizzling pieces of meat which she turned occasionally, crouched over the fire. When the meat was browned, she took it off the fire, poured a little *marc* over it and set light to it with a dramatic whoosh! of blue flame.

She transferred the meat into her *marmite*, a deep bulbous saucepan, on to a bed of vegetables – onions, carrots, potatoes, leeks – happily pouring in a good pint of red wine before adding the frying pan broth and setting the *marmite* to simmer over the fire. The delicious scents rose to a mouth-watering intensity.

We couldn't stay to sample it, but a spit-roast of *sanglier* was on the menu at our *réveillon*, an incredible 12-course New Year meal which we were still eating with the rest of the village at 3am. It was excellent, and nothing like its cousin, pork; a slightly gamey, dry meat, needing a lubrication of rich sauce. It reminded me of venison.

I don't know which suffered more, digestion or conscience. Conscience, probably. You can't work for years in primary education without becoming conditioned against hounding wild animals to death and letting 13-year-olds loose with shotguns. But perhaps we're not alone in struggling to accommodate conscience and appetite: at our local supermarket there's a collecting box shaped like a smiling pink pig. *Pour nos amis les bêtes*, it says, for our animal friends. Where is it? Yes, good question. Well, it's on the butcher-meat counter.

Now there's a moral tangle for someone to sort out. Someone with a clear view of things, unafraid to act on it. Someone like Sébastian, maybe?

Victoire! Victoire!

Beat the French at *boules*? Out of the question. We could give them a game, maybe, show willing, jack up the Entente Cordiale a notch or two. Or the Auld Alliance: after all, the challenge came from Scotland. But win? Impossible!

Boules? It's a kind of bowls, but much more ferocious and just as skilful, played with heavy gunmetal balls a bit bigger than a cricket ball which you bowl or lob through the air. There are two kinds of delivery, the *point* and the *tir*. The *point* tries to get your *boule* to rest as close as possible to the *cochonnet*, the jack. The *tir* is a high-speed delivery intended to cannon your opponents' *boules* out of the way, into the next *commune* if possible. Some people call the game

23

pétanque, but that's just its Sunday name. You can play it on almost any reasonably level and grass-free surface, and if there are bumps, stones and loose gravel, so much the better. It adds to the unpredictability and interest of the game. It's virtually the French national game. They play it everywhere, and our little village of Bardou is no exception.

The *piste*, or playing area, which was set aside for our France-Scotland *boules* match was on the edge of the village, just by Pierrot's wood pile, past Thérèse's house and over the little stone bridge, where the chestnut-shaded lane widens into the only flat area for some distance around, where the folk of Bardou have played *boules* for generations. Never before had they been able to boast of hosting an international.

There were just three of us, including myself, to represent Scotland: Tod and Ernie, on holiday with their families, were both noted sportsmen at home, Tod a mainstay of his golf club and Ernie scarcely ever parted from his skis in winter. But would their reputations travel? Would their sporting skills transfer to *boules*?

Scotland took the field complete with a trophy of malt whisky brought all the way from Speyside: a bottle of Tamdhu and a nice little quaich to drink it out of, to present to the French players Georges, René and César as the undoubted winners. The early evening sun shone, the crickets chirped, the village dogs Bigoudi and Pompon – and our own golden retriever Bellamy, now well enough integrated to be called a village dog – got in the way. The village turned out to watch, Pierrot among them, leaning against his wood pile, Gauloise in his mouth, with a roving eye much more attentive to the Scots womenfolk than to the play. All very pleasant, very French, *très sympa*.

Maybe a bit too *sympa*. Overcome by the occasion, by the drowsy perfumes of the sun-warmed earth, by the distant bells of the angelus, Scotland lowered its guard and allowed France to win the first of three ends 13–4. It was probably only by sending the Ernie-Tod daughters into the enemy's camp with plenty of beer that Scotland managed to pull the second end back, 13-10. Honours even. One round to go.

Were they rattled? Were Tod's sound eye and arm and Ernie's penetrating marbles-based technique beginning to tell? A tiny lead changed sides several times. With plenty of room round the *cochonnet* for a winning *point*, my *boule* slipped out of my hand while I was aiming and fell harmlessly at my feet. The chestnuts echoed with hearty French laughter. The rules are strict in *boules*; no prisoners taken, no quarter asked nor given. France 4, Scotland 3. A cannonball-like *tir* from René, a former artilleryman, endowed with a gunner's grim precision of trajectory, velocity and spin, scattered a promising Scottish lie and ricochetted on into the chestnuts, but *hélas!* carried the *cochonnet* to snuggle up against two otherwise unthreatening Scottish *boules*. Scotland 8, France 6.

The velvet evening wore on, the shadows lengthened, Georges, René and César fell unusually silent, brows furrowed in disquiet. Thérèse tapped her stick impatiently, Pierrot lit another Gauloise from the stub of the previous one, Pompon lifted his leg one last time and trotted off home. Crisis. A close-run thing, as the Duke of Wellington said of Waterloo.

But why prolong the agony? In the end we won the end 13-11 and the match 2-1. Handshakes, *félicitations* from Georges, René and César modestly brushed aside, our commiserations met with 'Ah, just you wait till next year. We'll show you . . .'

And then, a quite unforeseen embarrassment: we would have to present the trophy to ourselves. This difficulty was deftly side-stepped by Tod and Ernie; we would each take a quick victor's dram, and then present the almost intact bottle as a consolation prize, while I would be entrusted with the quaich, to keep bright and polished until the return match.

Weeks later, long after Tod and Ernie had taken their suntans and souvenirs back home, a much better arrangement occurred to me, in the way that might-have-beens do: surely Georges, René and César could have looked after the quaich, and I could have kept the whisky

...well, some you win, some you lose. But as for the *boules*, a famous victory. As Robert Burns would have said, if he'd been there, *From scenes like these old Scotia's grandeur springs.*

The Great Bardou Wedding

A few days before the Great Bardou Wedding Jean-Claude took me into his *cave*.

Jean-Claude, our neighbour, the doctor from Narbonne, is a small, round, good-hearted man, shaped liked a plump Kerr's Pink. He has so many prides and joys that it's difficult to know where to start listing them. Setting aside his daughter Sandrine, who rightly steals the scene later on, I could mention his 1974 Citroën estate (a DS, pronounced 'day-ess', i.e. *déesse*, meaning 'goddess'. Clever, *non?*) still in its prime. Or how about his enormous fund of *risqué* stories, a trait just as common among doctors in France as in the UK? His limited, but wholly practical command of English? ('Some wine, please?') His political courage, because he once stood as a right-wing candidate in traditionally red-hot, even Communist, Narbonne?

But at the wedding weekend his *cave* proudly came into its own. If you translate '*cave*' as 'cave' you're giving too much house-room to what my old French teacher used to call *un faux ami*, a false friend; *la cave* is the cellar, and by extension - like in English - the wine store. Visiting Jean-Claude's wine store involved much unlocking of creaking doors and creeping through low, cobwebbed passages until we arrived in an underground chamber, built of open stone and with a beaten earth floor, where it was wonderfully cool despite the torrid August heat outside.

There were uncounted bottles, hundreds and hundreds of them, red and white wines stacked shoulder to shoulder in the old mangers and feeding-troughs, relics of the days when *caves* used to house troglodytic goats and sheep; cases of champagne, goodly stocks of muscat, *pastis* (an aniseed-flavoured spirit, which turns white when you add water, like certain disinfectants, but there the resemblance ends), and a case or two of whisky, litre bottles with handsome blue, grey and gold labels reading Clan Campbell.

(Clan Campbell is a most useful whisky to me, because if I'm asked for my name I sometimes say, if a little ice-breaking seems appropriate: '*Campbell – comme le whisky*'. Like the whisky. Eyes light up. '*Ah, d'accord*', they say, spelling it out correctly instead of the usual COMBEL I get from those unfamiliar with Scotland's Finest; it's something they've heard of, even if no one in Scotland has, where it must be marketed under another name. '*Vous êtes de la famille?* You belong to the family?' they continue, smiling. '*Oui*', I reply unashamedly, glad my name isn't Laphraoig or Bunnahabhain, and the smile broadens: clearly I must be fabulously wealthy.)

I expected Jean-Claude to come out with a few philosophical remarks, even a *risqué* story, about the fleeting, here-today-gone-tomorrow qualities of such huge amounts of drink, but he was more concerned about whether there would be enough. After all, 400 guests were expected to the wedding. 400 guests in a tiny place like Bardou (permanent population: people 7, dogs 13)! Already the place was taking on a festive aspect, partly as the village parking area (room for 2 cars) was filled with flowers and tented over with bright awnings, and partly as streamers of red and white plastic tape sealed off the inhabitants' jealously guarded parking areas. Bardou is so up-and-down that every single near-flat space, even though there's only room for an elderly 2CV, is reverently handed down from generation to generation.

So The Great Wedding began to make its impact on the *escargot*-like advance of village chronicle. Years aren't necessarily identified by their number here, but by the events that occurred in them, and *les Bardousiens* have barely got over the last major event, The Year The

Wild Boar Ravaged Pierrot's Garden. The impact deepened as the first of the 400 began to arrive on the eve of the wedding. Bardou suddenly became alive with children running about and shouting, with groups gathered around guitars late into the indigo night, with cars with far-distant registrations creeping gingerly down the hill, wondering if this really was Bardou or just *Le Bout du Monde*, the end of the world: so much noise, excitement and animation that Justin's pack of hunting dogs, normally berserk with barking at the approach of strangers, slunk back into their kennels and, for all I know, covered their ears with their paws.

Picture the scene: normally Bardou lives at its own gentle rhythm, sunny summer days punctuated by a lizard running up the stone house walls, the tap of Thérèse's stick making her arthritic way up to her vegetable garden, the croak of a distant buzzard endlessly riding the mountain thermals, Pierrot singing *Petit homme, mets de l'huile* (Little fellow, oil it) as he starts his tractor, maybe Daniel the postman's van coasting down the lane noiselessly, so as not to set Justin's dogs barking. Then suddenly *PAF!* There are people everywhere, sleeping in tents and borrowed houses, shouting to one another in strange Northern accents, young people directing traffic to parking areas with walkie-talkies, bustle, movement, colour, excitement. *Inouï*. Unheard of, unparallelled.

The whole night before the wedding, it seems, there are bangings and singing, laughter and shouting, brought to a climax in the early morning by François, Sandrine's younger brother, a forestry student, enjoying his new toy, something else to shatter the peace of Bardou: a set of car horns which play *fortissimo* the opening notes of *Colonel Bogey*. Inevitably the time-honoured ditty about Hitler, Goering, Himmler and Goebbels comes into my head, and I make a mental note to tell Jean-Claude.

But on the wedding day there's no time for such diversions. As if *Colonel Bogey* isn't enough, there are distant rumbles of thunder, but these are quickly swallowed up in the constant to-ing and fro-ing, mostly directed by Sandrine herself, agreeably scruffy in T-shirt and jeans. I spend part of my morning rehearsing at the organ with Françoise, a pleasant lady who has come all the way from Geneva to sing at the wedding. She hasn't brought any music, but somehow we get by.

The hour nears, and I struggle into a suit that I've hardly worn since I left off being a head teacher several years and countless copious waistline-unfriendly meals ago. Suddenly the village empties, as the main party sets off for the Mairie, where M. Lemblay the *maire* is waiting to unite Sandrine and Franck beneath the plaster gaze of Marianne, the personification of France as Britannia is of Britain. The Mairie is in Les Verreries de Moussans, where the *salle de conseil* is so tiny that there's barely room for M. Lemblay and Franck and Sandrine, let alone the rest of the 400, who pack the narrow street outside, chatting, cheering, singing, turning a scornful eye on anyone vainly trying to drive through the village. How am I going to get to the church on time through the crowd? Luckily, with that homing instinct shared by church organists and undertakers, I know a quick way. Besides, they've entrusted me with the church key, so nothing can start till I get there. However, this sense of importance is rather undermined by being entrusted with Lucille too, an elderly and slightly infirm wedding guest with wonderfully developed powers of picking holes and grumbling. However, today she's all smiles as I guide her past the cemetery and as we settle ourselves in the cool of the church and wait for the invasion from the Mairie.

All goes well in a peculiarly French way. The *curé* welcomes the various nationalities – French, Spanish, Italian, English . . . I wait politely for him to move north of the Border before lifting my hand, but he passes on too quickly: Swiss, Slovenian, Belgian . . . little children run about and shriek, drowning Franck and Sandrine's promises . . . there isn't room for everyone in the church, and the crowd outside gets noisier and noisier . . . at the end there's an unseemly rush for the door, leaving the groom and bride to wander out by themselves, almost unnoticed.

At the sumptuous wedding banquet I find myself sitting opposite Lucille. She says she's tired, so I go and load her plate with good things from a groaning *hors d'oeuvres* table, but clearly she's back on form: there's too much of this, too little of that, why didn't I get her any gherkins, her favourite . . . the mountain ham hasn't been properly cured . . . *zut alors!* her glass is empty again . . .

Presently, between the courses (how sensible!) there's dancing, opened by the newlyweds with a Viennese waltz. I look on for a bit, until I feel something caressing my knee under the table. Opposite me Lucille, overcome by the ambience, is smiling archly, eyes twinkling . . .

Bardou has returned to normal now. I don't know about Lucille, but I'm not sorry.

Au Revoir, Bardou

I don't know what they must think of us, Thérèse, Pierrot, Emilie and the other neighbours. Nomads, tinkers, fly-by-nights, *gitanes* (gypsies) even. Here today and gone tomorrow. Shifty folk, always on the move.

I expect we flatter ourselves in supposing that they bother about us at all. And yet if a French couple suddenly turned up to live in some remote part of the UK, the Isle of Mull, say, it would be the talk of the neighbourhood, especially if after settling in comfortably they promptly disappeared.

As usual, the neighbours were very kind. '*Et alors, le voisin,*' Thérèse said, mock-severely: 'Now then, neighbour; you'll forget all about us and you'll never come to see us. What have we done to deserve that? Are we not nice neighbours?'

Francis, the retired railwayman, the communist from Narbonne (it's well known locally that Narbonne numbers more communists than Moscow ever did) who comes most weekends to stay in a doll's-house of a weekend cottage, about the area of a double bed – Francis couldn't understand our leaving: What was wrong with our house? Was it too big?

No, we said, it was fine, but it was uncomfortably cold in winter without central heating. The garden was pretty but really very small. We wanted land for a few sheep, woods for winter fuel, some chickens in the orchard, a strawberry bed, maybe a hive or two. This appeal to the *paysan*, to country roots as instinctive in Francis as in most Frenchmen, softened any extreme political reaction he might have had to our private ownership ambitions.

And Josie over the road, Josie the superb cook, said she would miss the sound of my piano, especially during the long summer evenings as she and her husband Jean-Claude sat out on their *terrasse* among the roses and buddleia. '*J'adore ça. C'est super-chouette*,' she said. 'I love that. It's really nice.'

We weren't going very far, in fact, just over the *département* boundary, out of the Hérault and into the Tarn: out of Josie's earshot, perhaps, but only about ten minutes away, down the lane to the modest town of Labastide, and a kilometre or two beyond, to a small farmhouse, *blotti*, to use a favourite French word meaning cradled or nestled, high in a wooded fold of these beautiful Languedoc hills, the last before the Mediterranean: La Prade Haute, The High Pasture, a stone-built house and about 10 acres of garden, grazing, woodland of oak and sweet chestnut, panoramic views south to the Montagne Noire, maybe the nearest to paradise we would ever get.

Buying and selling houses isn't much fun anywhere, but the French way has a straightforward and easy logic to it which compares favourably with the UK systems. How refreshing to have no solicitors, valuers, surveyors or building societies (the last two are virtually unknown here) with their plump fingers in the pie of property purchase! No estate agent either, because most local sales are by private treaty, although I wouldn't recommend trying this to anyone without a firm grasp of the French system and its legal jargon. To make up for any lost commission, we gave César Desjoyeaux, the St Pons estate agent, exclusive selling rights, unusual in France, over our house in Bardou.

So, a private deal, and a diet of pure adrenalin. Would M. and Mme Parmentier, the owners, accept our offer? If they did, how would we finance it? We visited them one evening, shivering with agonised excitement as our yellow headlights picked out the chestnut-lined drive and the old house at the top, windows lit softly and invitingly, almost seductively.

We made our offer, all we could afford, but still a monstrous amount less than the asking price in César's shop window. The words died in my mouth as they came out, and I knew it was useless. Why did we torture ourselves with such crazy ambitions? M. and Mme Parmentier exchanged heart-thumping glances . . .

'*Oui, d'accord,*' they said, unbelievably. No pause, no impatient frown at such a modest offer, no urging us to improve it. All those tenterhooks and goose-pimples for nothing. We could have kissed them with delight and almost tearful relief.

We formalised the agreement while it was still hot the following day at the *notaire's* office, and I paid the required deposit. (The *notaire*, a kind of public solicitor, has no equivalent in the UK.) The Parmentiers were now committed to selling to us, even if they received a better offer that afternoon, while we were legally bound to buy. Not quite inescapably: there's a sensible law in France which allows would-be buyers to withdraw if they can't raise a loan or mortgage. There was no need to invoke this, though, and on completion, after about eight weeks, we happily took possession.

So *bonjour*, La Prade Haute, and *au revoir*, Bardou. Thanks for all the good times.

LA PRADE HAUTE

Champignons, Grilled - Or Poached?

You can tell it's the mushroom season when ramshackle stalls appear in village doorways, a wicker basket on a chair, a couple of cardboard boxes leaning against the wall, with *CÈPES* chalked on a nearby plank. Hardly high-powered merchandising, but they'll be sold out by lunchtime. People stop, press and sniff critically at the huge bulbous mushrooms and choose the ones they want. Papy (grandad) shuffles out, a few coins change hands, and presently someone's kitchen will be richly scented with slices of *cèpe* frying lightly in olive oil with a little salt.

Mushrooms or toadstools? There's no such distinction here. They're all called *champignons*. People buy ordinary cultivated mushrooms, *champignons de Paris*, as a makeweight, perhaps to fill out a soup or an omelette, maybe to serve raw in a salad. However, they're short on flavour compared with many of the richly-prized wild *champignons*. The real mushroom buffs know where to find the tastiest ones almost all the year the round. Poaching isn't unknown, either.

The 10 acres of woodland and pasture at La Prade Haute thrive with beautiful *champignons* of every description. We seemed to be best endowed with St Michels, handsome parasol mushrooms wide as dinner plates. Why St Michel? I don't know. Perhaps it's because they appear at Michaelmas.

Like everybody else who knows where there's something interesting pushing its way up through the autumn leaf litter, we deemed it best to keep quiet about these riches. But we were novices, hardly able to tell a *girolle* from a *chanterelle*. Which were the edible ones? And could there be the Big One, the emperor of mushrooms, the *truffe* (truffle) of which people speak only in whispered reverence?

So we took our ignorance in hand, threw ourselves into a whirl of demonic energy, tramped the fields, collected 20 reasonably-sized varieties, consulted often quite contradictory guidebooks, threw out the obviously inedible or poisonous ones and took what was left to the chemist's.

This seemed an unusual thing to do, about as logical as taking fish you've caught for identification to the betting shop, but one of the more curious and endearing features of French country life is that High Street chemists are trained – otherwise they can't practise – to recognise *champignons*. M. Gasc, the chemist in Labastide, was our man: an elderly, shambling *pharmacien* who owned his own business and refused to retire from it, even though he was so short-sighted that he ran the risk of misreading *aspirine* for *arsenic* on the prescriptions his customers brought along from the doctor's and fervently hoped his assistant Régine would deal with.

(Maybe the idea would have appealed to him: for all his years he had an impish sense of humour. As the Labastide church organist he once unlocked the organ at the start of a rehearsal for a choir concert I was due to conduct. He sat at the organ bench, clicked and clacked at various stops and started to play the great Bach D minor Toccata and Fugue. His technique was impressive, he managed the resources of an electronic organ to their very best effect. Choir members arriving to rehearse stopped in their tracks, beguiled by the organist's mastery of this splendid music. Suddenly M. Gasc – still in his white chemist's overall – got up and walked out, flicking his bushy white eyebrows up and down like Groucho Marx, but inexplicably the music played on. He'd put on a demonstration track the organ was equipped with. You don't really expect this sort of jape from 80-year-old chemists.)

M. Gasc sorted through our collection with expert eye and nose, separated the gold from the dross and enthusiastically suggested ways of serving them. You can always count on extra large portions of enthusiasm when the preparation of food is the subject. If ever conversation with French people flags, you can inject new vigour into it by asking how they prefer things to be cooked. It never fails.

One of M. Gasc's suggestions was *beignets*, or fritters. He assured us that even the Giant Puffball was quite edible, if it was picked young enough, while the flesh was still firm and white. I had happy childhood memories of stamping on puffballs to see them erupt with a kind of thick brown smoke, and the idea of eating them seemed bizarre, at the least. But with M. Gasc's fritters you didn't have to look them in the eye, so to speak. You didn't have to agonise over plunging your fork into a slice of Giant Puffball when it was coated in a light batter. We found the flavour delicate, pleasant but nothing very special. But our St Michels! We tried one *en beignet*, and the flavour was deliciously succulent and savoury.

Another perfect, slug-free, dew-fresh St Michel, the first of a promising crop down in the as yet untenanted sheep field, found its way into the kitchen a day or two later, on a morning when M. Delbosc the electrician was struggling with a rebellious washing machine. He was enormously interested. He recommended grilling them, preferably *à la braise*, in the embers, with a little oil and a sprinkling of salt. '*On dirait bifteck,*' he said, his eyes sparkling. 'You'd say it was steak.'

This sounded more than interesting. The idea of a free and plentiful steak-substitute on the doorstep was certainly appealing. Tomorrow's lunch was just approaching perfection in the field. With a pair of binoculars we could see them growing from the kitchen window.

So could someone else, because the next day . . . but you've guessed it. Gone, the whole lot. Useless to threaten a 24-hour mushroom watch, useless to call on St Michael himself to avenge his own, to chastise with heavenly wrath the vile belly-driven greed of these miserable mushroom poachers . . .

. . . and when we had calmed down we found plenty more, better hidden and just as perfect. M. Delbosc was right. They were simply the most delicious mushrooms we'd ever tasted. *On dirait bifteck* indeed.

And the Big One, the fabulously expensive truffle? No luck yet. But then after the St Michel experience I've learnt to keep quiet about these things.

Baa, Baa, Mouton Noir

We counted thirteen sheep out of M. Gonzales' van, twelve assorted ewes, some of them yearlings, and an enormous ram with no manners, pushing and shoving his womenfolk about. A big beast as sheep go, Le Patriarche.

M. Gonzales had brought them in his old Renault van, which puffed its way up from Labastide and then up our drive to discharge its woolly passengers into our field. They blinked in the sunlight,

36

looked about themselves warily, and set to work at once to keep our foot-high grass down, which was the main reason for getting them. La Prade Haute means The High Pasture. We didn't want it to become The High Hayfield.

We offered M. Gonzales coffee, rather diffidently, because the French usually drink their fly cups of coffee, hot, strong and treacly black, in little beakers not much bigger than eggcups, while we, to our shame, have not yet abandoned our mugs of milky instant Nescafé or Maxwell House. We sat down in the shade of the big lime tree overlooking the field with its new occupants munching contentedly.

A hard-working but melancholy farmer, reminiscent of Eeyore in *Winnie-the-Pooh*, from the nearby village of Lacabarède, M. Gonzales is one of several local people with a northern Spanish or Catalan background, hence his name. Many, like his father, crossed the Pyrenees into France in the late 1930s, bedraggled escapees from the Spanish Civil War.

Our agreement was that his sheep would spend the summer and autumn at La Prade Haute, but that at the onset of winter he would take them back again. He would always be on call, he told me, if anything went wrong, and I was glad to hear it, because looking after sheep was something quite new to me. Even so, what he said was hardly reassuring.

'*C'est pas évident, les moutons,*' M. Gonzales told us, lugubriously. 'It's no joke, looking after sheep. They're born to die, you know,' he continued, a direct and unsentimental philosophy which I suppose all livestock farmers (and indeed many theologians) must share. I'd raced ahead to enthusiastic thoughts of the mint sauce before realising that M. Gonzales wasn't referring to the chief end of sheep, to keep us warm and grace our table (and, in our case, to crop our grass), but to their suicidal bent.

'If there's a stream, they're sure to drown themselves in it,' he said, gloomily. I was taken aback: a little stream tumbles and chatters down the field. In fact, it's our water supply, higher up, by the spring, where a contraption of roof-tiles, funnels and lengths of drainpipe, a kitchen sieve and a 5-litre mini-wine-barrel for a settlement tank provides a year-round supply of clean water.

'If there are cliffs, they'll hurl themselves off,' he continued. Worse and worse: the western edge of our land is cliff-bound, nothing very dramatic, but steep and high enough not to need fencing. M. Gonzales' disaster scenario continued. Trees? Where would they gather during our frequent thunderstorms? Under the tallest and most exposed. Parasites? They would lie all night in the tick-infested grass. Deadly nightshade? Mmm, tasty.

But he said nothing about my chief worry, the state of the La Prade Haute fences. Having lived so long in Scotland, I suppose we were conditioned to the hardy Scottish blackface, a breed skilled in the arts of escapology. You couldn't drive anywhere in the Highlands without coming across one or two bedraggled escapees. Our fences aren't nearly Colditz-like enough to resist Le Patriarche's determined heave, and then what trouble there would be: sheep run over, trapped in culverts, hounded to death, shot by hunters, stuck fast in drain grilles . . .

'Escape?' M. Gonzales said. 'Ah, no, no, no. They've got everything they need. They're in a family group, they've got good grass, fresh water, shade and shelter. They're perfectly content, Monsieur.'

Indeed they were. Perhaps we've been lucky. The grass is under control, the sheep show no interest in rock-climbing on the cliffs, they always cross the stream by the bridge, and we've had no thunder for weeks.

I'm perfectly content, too. Sentimental, even, especially on a summer evening, as the crickets prepare to sing into the starlit night and the declining sun gilds the top edge of the pasture where Le Patriarche and his flock lie peacefully chewing the cud. How does it go, that bit from *As You Like It*? 'I earn that I eat, get that I wear, owe no man hate, envy no man's happiness, content with my own harm; and the greatest of my pride is to see my ewes graze and my lambs suck.'

And the mint sauce? Yes, well maybe we'll put off thinking about that until tomorrow. *Demain*. Or as M. Gonzales might prefer, *mañana*.

From Russia, Avec Amour

Our involvement with M. Gonzales continued as agreed the next year, but took an unexpected turn when he brought his annual van-load of sheep one spring afternoon.

Some we'd had last year, he explained, before he uplifted them in December to pass the winter under cover in his *bergerie* in Lacabarède, but one old friend was missing: Le Patriarche was no more. For all his mass, muscle and moody masculinity, he had failed in his duty. Eleven ewes, only two lambs. *Pas bon*. So he had gone wherever sheep go after their last rendezvous with the butcher, unmourned by his virgin flock and unregretted by M. Gonzales.

'*Qu'est-ce qu'il*' – an alarming bit of French that comes out thankfully simply as 'kess-keel' – '*Qu'est-ce qu'il était méchant, ce voyou*,' M. Gonzales said. 'He was evil, that hooligan.' He showed me horrific scars on his hands and forearms where Le Patriarche had once pitched him into some barbed wire, admittedly after the sort of provocation you don't normally associate with the Good Shepherd, like being clouted over the head with a plank for being impotent. Let's move on quickly.

But the contents of his van weren't exhausted. There was someone else in it, a short, trim, petite blonde in her thirties, maybe half M. Gonzales' age, whom he introduced as Mademoiselle Irina from Russia, who couldn't speak French. I held out my hand and said '*Zdrazvitzye*', which has always seemed to me an unnecessarily complicated way of saying 'Hi'. Mademoiselle Irina's big brown eyes opened wide, and M. Gonzales almost smiled: '*Mais c'est parfait!* But that's perfect! You speak Russian!'

I had to admit that I only knew three words, and it was really just the luck of the draw that Mademoiselle Irina didn't get either of the other two, 'goodbye' and 'hedgehog'.

M. Gonzales unfolded a touching and poignant story, while Mademoiselle Irina smiled and bubbled her little pantomime of understanding beside him. One evening, cattle fed, sheep penned, dogs kennelled, poultry shut in for the night, M. Gonzales had settled by the fireside with no other companion but *Midi Libre*, the local paper, for a quiet but lonely hour before bedtime. His eye fell upon an advertisement of a Franco-Russian matrimonial agency, and who knows what romantic reveries curled upwards with the wreathed smoke from the oaken logs on the hearth?

Contact was made, and he and Mademoiselle Irina, neither able to speak the other's language, exchanged letters via a translator until deeper feelings stirred, and they began to feel shy about the translator playing gooseberry.

M. Gonzales could hardly leave his beasts, so Mademoiselle Irina arranged to leave Russia, which after all was her intention all along, and to brave the long journey to Lacabarède. She arrived the day before our sheep delivery with a French entry visa for a mere 28 days and a pressing need to find an interpreter to sort out the contracts that would enable her to drop Mademoiselle in favour of becoming Madame Gonzales. Could we help? We must know all the foreigners in the area, maybe even some other Russians?

We knew several non-French, it was true, and in fact since arriving in France we'd discovered unsuspected nests of expats; no Russians, however. But among French friends there was Marcel Têtu, an academic and minor poet, now retired from an active life which once included interpreting for the occupying powers – British, American, French, and most important, Russian – in post-war Vienna, like a bit part in the film *The Third Man*.

Nothing could give him greater pleasure, said M. Têtu when I called him, with the polite exaggeration that makes good French manners such a delight. Appointments were made and presently M. Gonzales was bidden *au revoir* and Mademoiselle Irina *dosvidanya* and they rumbled off down the drive, leaving us to our new intake of sheep.

After some weeks with no news from Lacabarède we began to fear the worst, that Mademoiselle Irina had outstayed her official 28-day welcome and had been *reconduite à la frontière*, led back to the frontier, the polite French way of saying deported. Then suddenly M. Gonzales and Mademoiselle Irina turned up with a thank-you present, a big crate of potatoes, and we heard the rest of the story.

M. Gonzales had made no effort to learn Russian in the meanwhile, but Mademoiselle Irina's French was coming on at a terrific rate. No romantic strolls in the warm summer twilight for her: as soon as work about the farm was done, the books were spread over the kitchen table, with eyes down for *j'aime, tu aimes, il aime, nous aimons* and so on. For the best of reasons: with M. Têtu's intervention, the French immigration authorities had agreed to extend her visa on condition that she and M. Gonzales married within a given period.

Over yet more milky instant coffee Mademoiselle Irina told us haltingly in her newly-acquired French that her mother was Russian Orthodox but her father was a Muslim; where she came from, Omsk in central Russia, such mixtures were common. It had taken her four days to reach Toulouse by train from Omsk, a journey which had cost her two and a half times her annual salary as a choreographer and teacher of dance. She'd saved for years for an eventual journey to the West.

The most surprising angle on this came from M. Gonzales. When he first contacted the matrimonial agency, they sent him thumbnail descriptions of over 4000 women as a starter. There were thousands more, mostly professional people, all looking to start a new life in the West. When he first took Mademoiselle Irina into one of the supermarkets in Mazamet, a modest town further down the valley, he was astonished when she burst into tears, weeping for herself and for the people she'd left behind. Never had she seen such enormous riches, such staggering, careless abundance.

The wedding was marked in an entirely appropriate way: our first lamb was born that day. We called it, in honour of Mademoiselle Irina's wedding promise in front of the *maire* of Lacabarède that afternoon, *Oui, l'ami* (yes, friend). North of the Border, of course, this would have come out as *Wee Lambie*. Clearly we left Scotland just in time, before they started throwing things.

To Market, To Market To Hear A Sad Tale

The market traders come back every Thursday, rain or shine, and we wonder how they can survive, what place there can possibly be for them in a retail world dominated by the supermarket giants.

Maybe the street market tradition is too deeply etched into the French soul to vanish completely in the face of such competition. At any rate in Labastide Rouairoux (the Rouairoux is added to distinguish it from the many other Labastides in the Midi), the depressed little town down in the valley a couple of kilometres from La Prade Haute, they evidently think the weekly *marché* has plenty of vigour left in it. It's by no means a rich place, but M. Tournier the *maire* and his council have invested a good slice of the annual budget in improving the market place and in building a large covered hall, modern and stylish, to shelter market traders.

Few tourists come to Labastide in search of local colour or bargain prices. If visitors to this area need a periodic fix of the colour and vibrancy, bustle and business and overall Frenchness of street markets, they go to nearby St Pons on Wednesdays or, hopeless addicts, to the wonderful Friday flower market in the tree-lined avenues of central Béziers. No, Labastide is a run-of-the-mill, homespun market serving local people, mainly elderly, who turn up week after week in denims and corduroys, greys, blues and blacks from the town, the surrounding villages and outlying farms. They all seem to know each other: it's as much a social as a commercial occasion.

It's hard to decide whether shopping or chatting is the chief activity as they mill about the stalls, among the fruit, hams and sausages, olives, strings of garlic cloves, shellfish from the Mediterranean, bolts of bright Provençal material, ironmongery, cheap shoes, kitchenware, army surplus and *bleus de travail*, the bright blue overalls typical of French peasants. All very practical and utilitarian. We join them sometimes and wander round, as intent on meeting friends and acquaintances as on actually buying anything. We exchange *Bonjour! Ça va?* with M. Célariès the pastrycook, smile at Mme Guermeur with her hill-pasture honey and M. Herbst with his goat's milk cheese; turn our tender northern eyes away from some live trout swimming disconsolately in a murky tank; pause, tempted for a moment by a woman selling a hen with a dozen tiny chicks peeping out from beneath her feathers, not something you could buy in a supermarket. We move on hurriedly. Chicks, like kittens, grow up.

And then at the next stall we're very surprised indeed to see an old friend, someone we haven't seen for several months: it's M. Gonzales, alone, selling home-grown vegetables. He looks older, greyer, even more melancholy. We ask how Madame Irina is. He shakes his head sadly, a man born for sad things to happen to. It has all been a tragic failure, he tells us.

Psychiatrists probably have a name for the condition Irina developed within days of marriage, and no doubt it had been incubating ever since she arrived in France. Her pretty blonde head, M. Gonzales says, was so turned by the riches of the West, by the superabundance of everything, that a mania for acquisition struck her irresistibly, like *un virus*. It had taken only a few weeks to empty M.

43

Gonzales' modest purse, and then, hooked on spending, she began to borrow and then beg for money from his friends. Worse, she . . . but he wouldn't weary us with all that. She'd gone back to her native Omsk. She wouldn't be returning. *Enfin bref,* in short, he was ruined. *C'est dur, la vie,* he says, life's hard.

We buy all his carrots – the least we can do – shake his hand sympathetically and move on, deep in thought. By midday the stallholders are packing up, and we go home too, unable to reach any conclusion about the Gonzales saga except that it's a shame. Maybe there was another side to it. There usually is. For a lively, bubbly Russian dancer, how did life on a smallholding in Lacabarède, perforce hitched to someone fairly well up the Eeyore ratings, match up to her early visions of it in distant Omsk? Maybe there's a Russian proverb, too, about the qualities of green-ness in grass.

Rain Of Terror

It sounded, improbably, like a juggernaut roaring up our drive in first gear at 9 o'clock at night, so I propped my dripping broom against the kitchen wall, put my cap and coat on, took the big golfing umbrella and our most powerful torch and stepped out into the downpour to see who'd come visiting on such an appalling night.

The drumming of raindrops on the umbrella was deafening, and the torch beam barely penetrated two metres through the pelting rain that had lasted two days and showed no sign of tiring. *Il pleuvait des cordes*, as they say, it was coming down like ropes.

No headlights, no engine ticking over, no cheery shouts of firemen come unbidden to pump our kitchen out. There was no one outside. Just as well: it was no night to be out in. Much better to retreat upstairs to the electric blanket before the electricity failed, as it usually does at the slightest upset to the general weather pattern. What was the point of staying up? Water kept coming into the kitchen through the back wall, where our house is built into the rock, faster than we could sweep it out of the door. Best let nature take its course. It couldn't rain for ever, could it? We would set to with brooms and mops again in the morning,

A horrifying thought – the roaring sound must have come from somewhere: suppose one, or several, of our terraces had given way under the weight of water and had tumbled down the hill in an avalanche of collapsed drystone walls, uprooted trees and mud? How safe was the house itself, built on a broad terrace scooped out of the hillside? I checked briefly. All the terraces near the house were so far intact, but it seemed sensible to move the car away – we have no garage – from any obvious avalanche threat. I went in, thoroughly shaken by the threats of disaster I'd invented for myself. There wasn't any need to scrape the mud off my wellies; the flow of water through the kitchen washed them clean in seconds.

In the morning the rain eased off after 60 hours of continuous downpour, the kitchen floor was almost dry, and the telephone started ringing. Solidarity, Dunkirk spirit calls mostly. There's nothing like disaster to unite people.

Up in the hills we'd got off lightly. On the coastal plain round Béziers there'd been loss of life and mass evacuations. Roads, bridges, livestock, caravans, whole vineyards had been washed away. The Hérault *département* had been declared a *zone sinistrée*, a disaster area. The President himself was coming to assess the extent of the flood damage.

Daylight showed the extent of our devastation. The surface of our steep drive had been almost entirely washed away, and our road end was impassably heaped with torrent-sculpted dunes of gravel, mud and tumbled lumps of tarmac. The *équipement*, the local council work-force, would clear the road with bulldozers in minutes, but for me there would be weeks of uphill work with shovel and wheelbarrow to repair the mini-canyons slashed down the drive, as though the tempest had ripped at it with giant claws.

And there, just on the other side of our little valley, was the explanation of the roaring we'd heard: a whole slice, a wide swathe of thickly-wooded hillside had fallen away in a giant waterlogged landslide, thousands of tons of rocks, mud and mangled trees, fanning out like a gigantic scallop where it reached the valley floor. Nothing could have withstood it. A narrow escape. It could so easily have been us.

Down in the hamlet of Mousse le Vieux, just the other side of the Atlantic/Mediterranean watershed where for once the weather had been equally hostile, Tall Agrippa the Dane had a different tale to tell. Mousse le Vieux is a place riddled with watercourses, above and below the surface, dry for most of the year, but even these couldn't cope with this downpour. Water sprang up in the night in his cellar, poured from cracks in the rocks in his garden, and the bridge over the ditch, like a small moat, in front of his house was awash beneath a wild torrent of muddy water.

That morning his neighbour M. Blasco came round partly to see how he had fared during the night but chiefly to introduce his latest acquisition, a West Highland terrier puppy they'd just christened Flocon. M. Blasco, shod only in trainers, was reluctant to wade over, especially with Flocon in his arms, so Tall Agrippa fetched a pair of boots and slung one over to M. Blasco.

It fell short, and was instantly washed away, lost to sight among the swirling rapids. It would reach St Pons in minutes, Béziers and the Mediterranean within a few hours. What use was the remaining boot? In a magnificently romantic, Hamletian gesture of propitiation to the gods of rain and flood, Tall Agrippa drew back his arm with poise and dignity and lobbed the other boot in too.

If the President found them during his visit, took them home to dry in the Elysée Palace and now pads about his garden murmuring *pas mal, ces godasses* (not bad, these boots), it never made the headlines of *Midi Libre*. But at least it stopped raining.

We were probably wondering what had induced us to settle in such a wet part of France one murky March afternoon when our attention was drawn to three cloud-shaped, ectoplasmic creatures looming out of the mist, moving purposefully up our drive. Out with the binoculars . . . sheep!

They weren't ours. We'd said farewell to our sheep the previous July, when the stream had dried up, no nourishment remained in the parched grass, and M. Gonzales took a quick break from his ill-starred matrimony to come and collect them. Whoever they belonged to, the first thing was to pen them, so with great patience they were wheedled into the field via the garden and a few passing bites of our prized polyanthi.

We rang our neighbours, an elderly couple called Viste who lived in the house end of an enormous stone barn a kilometre away at Le Castel: had they lost any sheep? Ah, *enfin*, Mme Viste replied, pronouncing it 'ahn-feng' as people do in the Midi, at last; they'd been lost for months, ever since the landslide. Did I know it had smothered their *abri*, their sheepfold, killing all forty sheep inside? I said yes, I knew, it was very sad. They'd bought another five, to start their flock all over again, but these had gone missing almost at once. Was I sure there were only three? Was one of them black? I peered into the misty gloom. Our visitors were head down, hard at it, metabolising our coarse grass into fine wool and mutton. One had a black face, not common here.

M. Viste would come directly he got back, Mme Viste assured us.

Presently there was a mighty, agonised bleating outside and ten more sheep appeared. The mystery deepened. On with the wellies, out with the long chestnut stakes that hold up our summer tomatoes. An ingenious tactical pincer movement, executed with Napoleonic

47

finesse, succeeded perfectly up to the moment when the field gate was opened; but instead of the newcomers going in, the original three escaped.

Reinforcements were called up in the form of our golden retriever Bellamy, who earned an extra supper helping of Pedigree Pal by simply lying across a temptingly grassy path into the endless woods behind the house. By the time M. Viste sputtered up the drive in his white Renault 4 van all thirteen were well and truly penned. It had taken a good hour.

He took one look at them, sighed deeply, and said *non*, they weren't his, but they were good sheep and they belonged to Mme Amalric, who has a weekend cottage and three acres down the hill. The Amalrics are much envied locally, because Monsieur, an engineer, has installed a mini-hydro-electric plant in his stream, by-passing the official Electricité de France supply, a scheme bound to appeal to any Frenchman engaged in the national pastime of putting one over officialdom.

(Are we going native? We feel the same about our private water supply, which bubbles and chatters out of the hill directly into our plumbing. It's beautiful water, the better for being free, and even the memory of once finding a leech hanging forlornly out of the hot tap when running a bath doesn't lessen the enormous pleasure of never receiving a water bill.)

But *revenons à nos moutons*. Mme Amalric, summoned from home in Mazamet, twenty-five kilometres away, picked her way up the storm-ravaged drive between the potholes *(nids de poule* – hens' nests – in French) in her new Renault Twingo. A smart lady, impeccably made up, she cut an incongrously *chic* figure among the nettles and barbed wire by the field gate. *Oui*, they were hers. *Mince alors* (probably the mildest French expletive), they must have broken out. They were great leaners, her sheep; once they found a loose fence post they would rock it until ˙ . . . in any case they'd overcropped her grass. They needed a change. The upshot was that her sheep stayed, keeping the spring grass down. A godsend.

As M. Viste said, they're good sheep, douce and biddable. It's becoming clear that Mediterranean sheep husbandry isn't the same as shepherding in the United Kingdom. There's no driving, for one thing, and not the same need for sheepdogs. These sheep follow, especially – *quelle surprise!* – music. I've only to put an old primary school recorder to my lips and whistle out *Mairi's Wedding* and they gather round at the gallop, and on we go in line astern to pastures new, especially if I have some stale bread in my pocket.

That's another problem solved, too, apart from keeping our grass down. We buy our daily bread from the lovely Patricia down in Labastide, a *baguette* usually or maybe a *flûte* if there are guests. It doesn't keep its gorgeous crustiness beyond a few hours, and there's always waste.

Or there was. They'll do anything for a mouthful of stale bread, these sheep, even listen to Step We Gaily, On We Go. It puts new meaning into the concept of The Good Shepherd. But all the same I wish we'd found M. Viste's sheep; one day, maybe, they too will turn up out of the mist.

The Barber Of Labastide

It seemed as good a way as any to start the New Year, to get my hair cut. 'God tempers the wind to the shorn lamb' has always been a favourite expression of mine, and in a largely sheep-based account of life at La Prade Haute a shearing wouldn't be totally out of place. Besides, I felt I owed M. Giméno, the Labastide hairdresser, a favour, because in pursuing the musical activities that have opened themselves up to me since arriving in France, every time I conduct a concert in the area he very kindly puts up a poster in his shop window. And not only that: he inks in jagged rainbows of fluorescent colour round the name CAMPBELL, brightening up the otherwise rather run-down Boulevard Carnot. Clearly a man to patronise. I only wish I had more hair to patronise him with.

There was no one in the shop the morning I called, but after coughing pointedly once or twice and finally calling out '*Y a quelqu'un?*' ('Shop!') Mme Giméno put her head round the house door and said her husband had just gone to see his *député*, his MP, and could I please come back at 2.30? Indeed, parked not far away in the Place des Maquisards was a big bus, painted all the colours of the major French political parties. Along the side was inscribed *Permanence de Bernard Carayon, député du Tarn* (it isn't too easy to translate *permanence*, but whenever you see it it means someone's there occasionally) and as I passed by there seemed to be a minor French political party taking place inside. At any rate there was a lot of laughter and clinking of glasses.

At 2.30 the salon, otherwise faultlessly clean and tidy, was streaked with a noisome smoke: M. Giméno was singeing the cropped head of the previous customer with a candle. Wondering if I hadn't made a serious error of judgement, I sat down and took a magazine to glance through while waiting. But I couldn't concentrate: watching an artist like M. Giméno at work was too compelling. He'd stuck the candle in a funnel, to prevent any drips scalding the near-hairless pate, and was blowing delicate tongues of flame hither and thither, seemingly in complete control. The customer, possibly a soldier, looked in the back mirror, murmured '*impeccable*', paid up and left. My turn.

Sat in the chair, robed and collared like a Pope or a Grand Inquisitor, I sensed M. Giméno planning his attack. The truth was that I hadn't been to the barber's for more than 25 years; there isn't much to cut, and what there is has always been done at home. 'Ah well,' he said finally, and doubtfully: 'suppose I just *arranged* Monsieur's hairs?' He set to work with comb and scissors and I waited for his barber's patter to start. Would it be the weather? The Labastide football team? President Chirac's New Year address?

It was nothing so predictable. He started talking about the acoustics in local churches. He seemed to have an encyclopaedic knowledge. Yes, he would be coming to the concert advertised in his window. He was very fond of good sacred music. He knew the exact spot in the church where the sound was perfect. I was sorry it was too late to put an extra credit in the programme: *Coiffeur de M. Campbell – William Giméno* with GIMENO surrounded by a jagged halo of felt-tip pen colour.

I asked him about his visit that morning to Bernard Carayon. Had it gone well? Very, very well, he said. *Très, très bien.* M. Carayon came to Labastide to hold his surgery once a month or so. His bus was fitted up with an office, a small auditorium, a private consulting area and a bar. Had he a particular point to make to M. Carayon? I asked. No, he said, he just went for the *apéritif* (i.e. the drink) and to tell M. Carayon how he saw the future of Labastide panning out. Something would have to be done: the population was ageing, in less and less need of hairdressers. In the country of the bald the one-haired man might be king, but it was a bad look-out for barbers. In short, his business was for sale, and M. Carayon had promised to put him in touch with a relocation agency in Paris, serving people who wanted to buy small businesses in the Midi.

I knew what was coming next, as he gently disposed of a few stray clippings from my neck with a car hoover and pocketed his fee. It was as predictable as his patter about church acoustics had been surprising. Did I know anyone in my country who might fancy starting a new life as a gentlemen's hairdresser in a sleepy village in the south of France? I promised to pass it on. Commission? Yes, I'd take a commission: a free haircut every now and then. Not often. Maybe a little more often than once every 25 years, though.

The Bottleologist

Today M. Robert the *facteur* has left something new in our post box. It's a tabloid-size newspaper, 12 pages long, well printed on good paper. *Les Petits Thoréliens*, it's called, which doesn't translate very easily: The Little Ones from the Valley of the Thoré. The Thoré, not one of France's loveliest rivers, links our village of Labastide with other villages further downstream, Lacabarède and St Amans, before reaching the town of Mazamet on its eventual way to the Bay of Biscay.

It turns out that the Little Ones are the primary schoolchildren of the valley, and this is their bi-annual newspaper, distributed free to every household in the district. The main theme of this issue is Written Communication, and pride of place is given to a M. Jean Batut, a pensioner from Béziers, whose hobby, surely not a common one, is putting messages of goodwill with a prepaid reply coupon into plastic bottles weighted with a little sand, and launching them into the Mediterranean to seek their fortune. And not just the Mediterranean; his passion has taken him much further afield, the Canary Islands, Tahiti, Australia and even Scotland. Sadly, the bottle he consigned to the dark waters of Loch Ness has so far brought no return of Caledonian goodwill. Maybe it's still bobbing up and down in Drumnadrochit Bay.

M. Batut the *bouteillologue* – which I suppose you could translate as 'bottleologist', but I wouldn't care to meet either word on a dark night any more than a Petit Thorélien would care to meet them in a spelling test – had been invited to Labastide primary school to give a talk, illustrated with maps and fascinating statistics:

Bottles launched: more than 1000.

Replies to date: 197

Record bottle speed: 50km per day

Swiftest reply: 16 days, from Algeria

Slowest reply: 993 days, also from Algeria

Proudest moment: a bottle-launch from the French aircraft carrier *Foch*

Oldest bottle-friend (that doesn't look quite right, but you know what I mean): Georghiu the Albanian shepherd.

After talking to the children M. Batut oversaw the preparation and launch of several bottles, each containing the children's messages of friendship, before a stiff off-shore breeze towards the blue Mediterranean horizon and distant lands beyond. Where might they end up? Sicily? Majorca? Malta? Egypt?

A month later the first reply came in, from a place called Sidi-el-Bechir, near Bizerta in Tunisia. Huge excitement, good learning, and friendly contacts established, and there aren't many things more important than that.

Another report in *Les Petits Thoréliens* featured a very different Written Communication correspondent, from overseas again but this time north of the English Channel. The local schools, acting together, chose the conventional post, snail-mail rather than M. Batut's bottle-mail, to send a message of greeting and congratulation to Queen Elizabeth on her 70th birthday. As a little present they sent her some recipes of typically French dishes, *pour régaler le palais de la reine d'Angleterre*, to tickle the Queen of England's palate, a kind and touching thought.

In due course M. Robert the *facteur* delivered the Queen's letter of thanks, which Les Petits Thoréliens proudly reproduced in full, including the envelope, addressed with scant regard for capital letters but with all the accents meticulously marked in by hand by the Buckingham Palace secretariat: *The Queen has been most interested to see your delicious recipes . . .*

We weren't told what the recipes were, but Her Majesty may have been well advised to see them rather than try them. Elsewhere in *Les Petits Thoréliens* there's a recipe for *Cake au thon*, i.e. Tuna Cake, a concoction of flour, olive oil, eggs, milk, grated cheese and tuna. We haven't tried it either, but it probably rates as highly on the Franco-British gastronomic ladder as toad-in-the-hole or stovies. I'm sure M. Batut would be delighted to forward copies of it, on request, but there could be some delay before they actually arrived.

A Passing Show

The posters had been up for a day or two, lashed to all the Labastide lamp-posts, announcing the imminent arrival of *Vacherie camarguaise*, ninety fun-packed minutes' worth of Frolics from the Camargue.

We know the Camargue slightly, an extraordinary place about three hours' drive from here. It's the delta of the river Rhone, a vast flat area of wetlands known for its pink flamingos, rice growing, wild horses and cattle, especially bulls, and the last two have combined to produce a kind of Mediterranean cowboy-cum-matador culture. But *vacherie?* Frolics?

I was collecting our daily *baguette* from the lovely Patricia in Buso the baker's when a slowly-driven publicity van, reinforcing the message of the posters, shattered the usual lazy peace of the Boulevard Carnot. Bursts of urgent, macho Spanish music split the air, and presently a mighty voice with a fruity, bubbling accent announced *all the thrills and spills of the arena in* – there was a long pause: maybe the mighty voice wasn't too certain where it was, or maybe Labastide Rouairoux was too much of a mouthful – *in your town tonight, in the field opposite the Peugeot garage.* The voice, promising prizes for amateurs, Doppler-shifted away, mighty no longer, and the *paso dobles* tinkled off into the distance.

The posters showed vast crowds, the population of Labastide many times over, surrounding a circular pool with a 3-metre wide deck round it. A massive bull, snorting ferociously, was depicted charging round the deck, and any amateurs not nimble enough to win a prize by dodging it could only escape a nasty mauling by leaping into the water. We were promised other delights: there would be donkey and pig races, too.

At this point I should admit that this account is seriously flawed, because that night, being promised elsewhere, a long way away from the field opposite the Peugeot garage, we never got to see the Frolics. We wouldn't have gone anyway, from choice. The Mediterranean passion for capering about with bulls may stretch back into the remotest pre-history (think of the Lascaux and Altamira cave-paintings, think of the Minotaur legend in Crete), but it collides head-on with our soft Northern susceptibilities. However, it isn't often that a sleepy little place like Labastide has its own *feria* or bull-fight festival, so I did the next best thing; in the afternoon, while they were setting up, I waved my press card and asked for *le patron*.

A surprised M. Chansegrand, a lean and pinched man, said there was no *patron*, it was just a little family business. We sat on the lowest tier of the stand and watched as other Chansegrands erected a security fence round a grassy arena where several very small bulls about the size of reindeer were grazing peaceably. Tethered beyond was a solitary donkey. In a little pen two pigs slumbered in the sun. The fire brigade was coming later to fill what looked like a childrens' paddling pool.

M. Chansegrand was in a nihilistic mood. Everything was *pourri*, rotten. He couldn't carry on. Nobody came to see his show any more. Did I know how many people came to the last performance? Seven. No, he didn't come from the Camargue. He belonged to Clermont Ferrand, many miles to the north, but he spent all his time travelling. At the Mairies, where you had to ask permission to perform, they were treated like *bohémiens*, gipsies – worse, even: they were treated like Arabs.

Hurriedly changing the subject, I asked what his animals were called. His two best, Réquita and Paquita, he described as *vachettes* rather than *taureaux*, bulls, and indeed they were just stirks, slim and glossy, and with protective ribboned caps over the tips of their horns. The solitary donkey was called Martin Zébulun.

Where was my paper based, he asked: was it Albi? No, I said, it was published in Scotland. Ah, he'd heard it was a rich place, Scotland. Would they be much interested in his Frolics? I said I didn't think so, but many Scots loved France and French life. More fools them, he said. France was finished. He hadn't much schooling, but he knew what was what. In the old days the aristocrats lived in their *châteaux* and if you had two hens they took one and you grinned and bore it. Nowadays it was much worse. *Oui*, maybe there was more *liberté* to sit in the sun, like we were doing then, but there was precious little *fraternité* and as for *egalité* . . . if you had two hens, the government took all the eggs.

I shook his hand and left. Early next morning, before 8 o'clock, I drove past the field opposite the Peugeot garage. It was empty. Not a sign remained of M. Chansegrand and his *vacherie camarguaise*. A shame. I would have liked to ask him how it had gone the previous evening. Not well, I daresay. I suspect the only winner may have been Martin Zébulun.

PEOPLE

Unlucky Strike

I went to see César Desjoyeaux, the estate agent, and found him plunged in gloom. He has a tiny shop in the middle of St Pons, just along from the cathedral square. César is a minimalist: there's nothing in his shop except three odd hard chairs and a desk supporting a telephone, a jam-jar for pens, and César's elbows as he stares balefully at passers-by, chin cupped in his hands.

As a concession to décor and customer well-being there are two postcards on the wall behind him, a view of Shrewsbury and an early photograph of William Morris, both sent months before by British clients. No smart secretaries or smiling receptionists. There isn't room, for one thing. If several customers arrive at once, the overspill has to wait outside, by the climbing rose which has somehow taken root in the paved gutter between César's shop and the *boucherie* next door.

I squeezed in on a perfect autumn morning, and it was clear that all was not well. I asked him if he was *un peu fatigué*, out of sorts. No, César said, pressing his stomach tenderly, he was all right apart from feeling a little empty. Was he *fou furieux*, then, in a towering rage? It wasn't as bad as that, he said. He was just *vexé*.

I saw it all, or thought I did. That day France had been brought to a near-standstill by a strike of *fonctionnaires*, public sector employees. There was little public transport, schools were closed, mail was undelivered and even the St Pons Mairie was closed for the day. César had decided views about a body politic that allows *fonctionnaires* the luxury of striking while humble *commerçants* like himself have to struggle every minute of the day to put two *sous* together. In fact he's in a permanent state of protest against the government, which he expresses in a particularly individual way.

'I never vote,' he says, waving a warning finger at me, as though I was personally responsible for the ills that beset France. 'And nor should you. It only encourages them.' If you think this is just a silly cop-out to save himself the trouble of voting, I can only wish you better acquaintance with César: on polling day he'll be among the first to appear, presenting his *carte d'identité* and demanding his ballot paper. He'll take it into the polling booth, where he'll fold it carefully in four, emerge and drop it with dignity into the ballot box, looking straight into the eyes of Marianne, the personification of France, whose plaster *tricolor*-sashed bust in every Mairie sternly reminds Frenchmen and Frenchwomen of their civic duty. When the votes are counted, César's anonymous, unmarked, virgin paper will join the large pile of abstentions.

When you talk it all over with César you stray some distance from the comfortable, tourist vision of France, the sunny, placid, rich land where contented peasants tend the vines between the siesta and the evening game of *boules*, while the angelus rings from the village steeple and the smiling girl at the *boulangerie* . . .

'*N'importe quoi*,' César says impatiently. Twaddle. The tourists'll be lucky if the Loire isn't running with blood, if the mob isn't tearing down the hated Eurodisney for missiles to storm the European Parliament at Strasbourg with, or vice versa, if the Corsicans . . .if the Breton fishermen . . . if the railwaymen . . . if the pensioners . . . if the Arabs . . . if the National Front . . . 'and when everything boils over, plunging France into Revolution,' César says, wagging a doom-laden finger again as he works up to his apocalyptic climax, 'it won't be on my conscience, it won't be my fault, because I looked Marianne in the eye *and I didn't vote.*'

This was all very well, but I didn't think it entirely explained César's vexation that morning. I came back to my original scenario. César's wife Annie is a *fonctionnaire*: she's first secretary at the Mairie. Perhaps there had been some awkwardness, perhaps stances had been taken, even words exchanged, in the Desjoyeaux household that morning. Such was my thesis.

'Bof!' César said, an interjection of infinite scorn. She could do what she liked. Liberty of conscience was the hallmark of civilisation, even it if it did mean that Annie stayed in bed while he went down at 7.15 that morning, as he had done for the last 20 years, to the *boulangerie* in the Route de Narbonne for his daily bread and a *pain au chocolat* for his breakfast and had found them sold out. Imagine. Sold out. At that hour of the morning. Scandalous. Those *fonctionnaires* had a lot to answer for.

Fonctionnaires? I asked. How could they possibly have anything to do with it? They were on strike.

Et comme quoi, César said. Some strike. They'd just ganged up to help themselves to a day off. Perhaps I hadn't noticed that France, or the Midi at least, was in the grip of its annual mushroom fever? Any edible mushroom or toadstool that popped its head above the parapet was liable to be picked off by the swarms of *champignon* hunters that throng the local oak and chestnut woods at weekends in autumn.

So that morning postmen from Montpellier, tax officials from Sète, teachers from Béziers, railwaymen from Narbonne had thrown back the shutters, had seen what a beautiful day it was, and had all with one accord bundled the kids (there was no school, after all) into the car and had headed north towards St Pons, to the hills and the woods in the hope of enough *cèpes* and *bolets* to satisfy the inner *fonctionnaire* for days to come. And where had they stopped on their way, very naturally, to buy *pains au chocolat* for their in-car breakfasts and bread for their *pique-niques*? Why, at the *boulangerie* in the Route de Narbonne.

So César went hungry, and I hoped he wasn't counting on *cèpes* at lunchtime. I too had a problem, in my own small way: I didn't care to admit that I'd been a *fonctionnaire* once, before coming to live in France. Not at breakfast-time, anyway.

Going For A Song

A blazing July day takes us along the valley of the Jaur, one of the most beautiful and least-known rivers of the deep South, to see a remote hamlet for sale, mostly in ruins, lying on a hillock in a herb-scented navel of the Languedoc hills. It has no connection with the half-village we nearly bought a year or two back, and we're not seriously interested unless everything, price included, clicks into place. We're what César calls *promeneurs*, people who go about looking at properties they've probably no intention of buying, but you never know until you've looked at a place . . . in any case it's not on César's listings, so we haven't troubled him with it.

It turns out to be a dream-like enchantment, a magical, seductive place, a paradise, lazily vibrant with the summer music of distant crickets and cicadas and the trickling of the spring into a *bassin* where berry-brown children play from dawn to velvet dusk. Fancy owning a whole village! It belongs, every stone, pepper-pink tile and sun-bleached shutter, to a Mme Moustaki. She's spent years, ever since she arrived from Paris, buying every surrounding plot of land, vineyard, patch of *garrigue*, Mediterranean oak thicket and bramble patch. Now, just as it all belongs to her, she wants to leave. She's getting on: in summer time the living is easy, but winter's another matter.

The name Moustaki tinkles a faint, distant bell. Where have we heard it before?

She's made a parking area out of the old village threshing-floor, exposed rock polished smooth with generations of flailing and winnowing. Peaches and nectarines hang from drooping branches. Lizards scuttle away into an untidy vineyard, whiskery for lack of winter pruning, with tight green clusters of grapes the size of peas. Awns of bleached grass in the middle of the lane stick in our socks.

How many buildings? Impossible to say. Ten or twelve? The shapeless hump overgrown with wild clematis might have been the village bread oven, a bramble thicket might hide a *secadou*, a chestnut drying kiln. A tiny house, one up, one down, has a door in the shape of an egg. Mme Moustaki calls it the *garçonnière*. It's for visiting lovers. We tiptoe past, just in case. Idylls shatter so easily.

Two adjoining houses look reasonably habitable, with electricity cables and new roofs. An ancient kitchen, smoke-blackened, hung with netted hams, strings of onions and bunches of herbs, leads into premises confirming that Mme Moustaki is *une originale*: we're in for a surprise. A smartly decorated gallery, like a long mezzanine, alcoved with areas for reading, chatting, sleeping, writing and the storage of thousands of books, looks down into the heart of the house, a replica of a Paris *bistro*.

Here, among the cast-iron tables, black and white floor tiles, hoop-backed chairs, ashtrays labelled Byrrh or Suze and the sharp, sweet tang of Gauloises, Mme Moustaki sits in henna'd and faded glory, dispensing *apéritifs* or coffee from an asthmatic machine, but chiefly a fascinating nostalgia for the 1950s and the café society of Jean-Paul Sartre, Simone de Beauvoir . . . and Edith Piaf.

Suddenly it clicks. She's the wife (ex, it turns out) of Georges

Moustaki, no mean singer himself, who wrote the lyrics of the greatest of the Edith Piaf songs, *Milord*. Remember? *Allez, venez, Milord, vous asseoir à ma table* (Come on, Milord, come and sit at my table). I shouldn't be surprised if doctoral theses at obscure American universities hadn't been written about this song and its symbolism.

But Mme Moustaki is more interested in her own creations, writing and making jewellery, than in somebody else's old songs. And in selling up: *vaut mieux vieillir à Paris qu'au Paradis*. It's better to grow old in Paris than Paradise. Who knows? Maybe she's right.

Can the sad-eyed Mme Moustaki see her overgrown Garden of Eden, *garçonnière* and all, weaving its enchantment about us, like *Milord* in the song? We ask her price: it's steep by local standards – although an absolute snip compared with UK Home Counties or up-market US prices – even with a few quavers of French musical history thrown in. Too much for us: we make our apologies and leave.

A few months later we hear that there's been a fire, and the habitable parts are now in much the same state as the rest of it. Mme Moustaki is unhurt, but she's lost much. Perhaps this is why the price has gone up. Clearly memories, even charred ones, are dearer than dreams.

Distance No Object

In the early 80s I glanced sometimes – as a parent – at my children's first year French course. Part of it revolved round the antics of removal men based in Créteil, an unlovely Paris suburb. It's never easy, of course, to engage the total interest of twelve or thirteen-year-olds in French language and life, and I used to wonder how gripped my two were by the witless *déménageur* who asked *c'est une table?* only to be told by his long-suffering gaffer *non, c'est un fauteuil*, no, it's an armchair. You have to start somewhere, I suppose. But removal men?

However, another phrase stuck, a useful formula for asking the way, and I remember gasping it out once, panic-stricken in the desperate jungle of junctions and road signs in the middle of Rouen. I hailed a passer-by: *Pour aller à Evreux?* Unusually obligingly for a Frenchman bawled at by a passing Brit, he pointed in the direction I was already heading in and shouted above the roar of traffic *tout droit*, straight on. Thirty minutes later I was in Evreux, eager to test the pro-Britishness of the populace by shouting *pour aller à Dreux?* – the next town down the holiday route to the Midi – if the local road signs weren't up to much.

Some of this came to mind when I had to take two beds from Olargues, the very pretty village where my Languedoc wanderings have finally led me, to Agel, another village 45 kilometres away in the Minervois, an area carpeted in thick-pile vineyards whose name may be familiar from supermarket wine shelves or, better, from the tilted label as the bottled sunshine colours your glass.

When it comes to shifting furniture in Olargues, there's only one man: Claude Lauze. Whatever the name Claude may suggest in other parts of the world, our Claude is tall, lean, muscular and bronzed, a rugged 40-year-old *galant*. The call to shift two beds brought him putt-putting up in his battered 1973 Renault 4L bursting with demonic energy, such a valuable quality in a general handyman.

Claude has worked in his time as a France Télécom linesman, quarryman, forester and drystone wall builder, besides tending his own vineyards and cherry orchards; heaving two substantial sky-blue beds and their mattresses on to his roof rack was child's play. Having tied them on to useful projections like door-handles and petrol tank caps with – what else? – bits of frayed baler twine, we jolted off in the direction of Agel, lurching top-heavily, so that you could feel the centre of gravity shifting at each bend.

Claude chatted away about one of the projects he usually has on the boil. He was thinking of producing his own wine under his own label. At present he sent his grape harvest down to the *cave coopérative*, but his grapes weren't special and he didn't get much for them. He didn't know what happened after that; his wine was probably tankered off to Spain to be mixed with other lowly vintages, shipped to Italy for further mixing and finally exported to Timbuktu, for all he knew. His vines, passed down from father to son, were old, and the varieties, Carignan and Grenache, produced a thin, acid wine, the very stuff of what used to be called 'plonk' (a corruption, some say, of the 'blanc' of *vin blanc*) in the days when massive over-production of poor quality wine led to such follies as the European Wine Lake.

Claude was finding himself caught up in the improvement that has revolutionised wine production in the Languedoc. He already had his own *cave* with its enormous *fûts*, wooden fermentation barrels. He planned to grub up the more pensionable Carignan and Grenache vines, planting in their place Merlot and Mourvèdre, varieties which bring out and round off the flavour and body, like salt and spices in cooking, transforming a nasty wine into something much more enjoyable.

I asked him what he would call his wine, remembering that I once came across a pleasant *rouge* called Château Mourel, which originated from St Nazaire de Ladarez, a village hidden in the folds of the Languedoc hills north of Béziers. A dinner invitation took us there one day, and looking about as we entered the village, half-expecting a handsome Languedoc *château* with slated turrets and a green sea of vineyards lapping its balustraded terraces, I was surprised to find that M. Mourel's *château* was in fact his garage. Château Lauze? I suggested, even though Claude doesn't have a garage but parks his modest fleet of beat-up cars and vans wherever he can find a space around the village.

However, development of this topic was interrupted as we approached St Pons by cars flashing their lights at us, warning us of a police checkpoint a little further on.

Claude pulled in smartly. His papers were in order, but our load would never pass a police check. Baler twine, indeed. There would be an instant PV, *un procès-verbal*, an on-the-spot fine, points deducted from his licence, the beds confiscated. *Eh bien*, Claude said, grinning broadly at the prospect of a new challenge: *Pour aller à Agel?*

A good question. Our road lay through St Pons, where four valleys meet, a town of important local road junctions. Maybe we should just wait for *les flics* to go, I suggested. In a sleepy place like St Pons all work, even manning checkpoints, stops for lunch on the stroke of midday; it should be safe enough then. But Claude had other ideas. It was only 10.30, and he for one wasn't going to waste an hour and a half of a perfect autumn morning skulking about in a lay-by. Suppose we took a mountain road he knew? We turned round and picked up a single-track road whose hairpin bends took us up about 700 metres, on one side rocky cliff where clumps of heather and wild fig trees cling, and on the other an almost sheer drop.

Up and up we climbed, until the distant Pyrenees rose above the forests on the other side of the valley, and St Pons with its cathedral and checkpoints cheated of their prey dwindled to Lilliput-size far below; although I had only eyes for the mini-avalanche of sky-blue bedsteads and mattresses threatening to hurtle down the precipice with every lurch.

So we skirted St Pons in a 25-kilometre detour, arrived in Agel and delivered the beds undetected by *les flics*, an hour later than planned. Mission accomplished. What would the school French course removal men would have made of our outing? *C'est un lit?* Is it a bed? *Non, c'est un secret.* You wouldn't have given us away, would you?

Question: How do you get rid of an old electric cooker, a dead lawnmower, some immensely heavy sacks of blown plaster, an old carpet supporting a thriving ecosystem, half a pair of antlers and a red plastic savings hippo – empty, of course – labelled 'Bank of Scotland'?

Answer: You put them all in the trailer and take them along to the St Pons dump.

Easier said than done. There was a big notice at the dump entrance saying *For the use of local residents only, by Mayoral decree. Unauthorised users risk prosecution.* Strong stuff. Unfortunately, we weren't local residents. St Pons is in the Hérault *département*, and we'd recently moved to La Prade Haute, in the Tarn *département*, just over the border. Hence the need to clear out. Never mind that the St Pons dump is the nearest and best-run for miles around: everyone in France carries an identity card, so you can't bask in anonymity, or pretend you come from St Pons when your card says quite plainly that you don't.

Still tentative about these things, not yet feeling quite confident enough about living in France to assert myself in the gung-ho, just-do-it way that many Frenchmen run their lives in, I consulted Jean-Claude Ghisgant, our weekend neighbour in Bardou. Car number-plates were the problem, he said. If you had 34 on the end of it, showing you were registered in the Hérault *département*, no one would raise an eyebrow, but with my 81 plates, showing I came from the Tarn, *eh bien*, you never knew what attitude they might take. Things could turn out quite nastily . . .

They? I asked. Who were 'they'? Security guards? Bouncers? Vigilantes? No, Jean-Claude said, but he'd gone once with a load of rubbish and received a really disagreeable mauling from a St Pons councillor who happened to be there. Jean-Claude's number plate, sporting 11 for the Aude *département* where he lives when he's not at

Bardou, had given him away. In fact, he'd been seriously *invectivé*. This wasn't a word I knew. It sounded painful.

Despite Jean-Claude's misgivings I set off, with the trailer bouncing along down the winding hill road to St Pons, giving the carpet-dwellers a long overdue shake-up. At the dump entrance there were no pickets of muscular bin-men, menacingly fingering stout staves: so far, so good. I drove down to a freshly levelled area, where three men, the digger driver and two bin-men, were trying to wrench open the drawers of an old office desk some law-abiding St Ponais had dumped.

I recognised one of them, a burly youth with glasses mended with sellotape, which they call 'scotch' here. I knew his granny, Marcelle, a plump and pleasing person who sang in the front row of the altos in the choir I conducted at that time. My glaring 81 number plates earned a passing glance, but no comment.

Going for broke, I asked where I should empty my trailer. The burly youth answered with that impeccable but distant politeness that *gendarmes* are supposed to use before they fine you, if necessary frog-marching you to the nearest cashpoint: 'If Monsieur would care to look up there, by those oildrums, in the brambles?' I followed his outstretched arm towards an overgrown hillside patch on the edge of the dump, accessible only by mountain goat. Or maybe by parachute.

So that was it. A cruel trick. I should have paid more attention to Jean-Claude. Idiot, imbecile, to think I could buck the system. But the burly youth hadn't finished: *'Si ça ne vous dérange pas* – if you don't mind, Monsieur – that is the only place where we would prefer you not to put your rubbish.'

I started unloading and presently there was a modest cheer. The three men had succeeded in bursting open the last drawer of the derelict desk and had found the hoped-for unconsidered trifle to snap up: an unused France Télécom card still in its cellophane wrapper. I don't know whose way this bounty went. Perhaps they have a turn-about system for bin-men's perks.

Seeing me struggle with the sacks of solidified plaster, he came over and effortlessly lifted them out of the trailer for me. A little something to say *merci* seemed called for, so I searched my pockets for change. In vain: all I had was the red Bank of Scotland hippo, so I gave him that.

I looked up *invectiver* when I returned home. It wasn't as bad as I thought. It means to insult, to bad-mouth. I was surprised, all the same: Jean-Claude is too pleasant and well-mannered a person to deserve verbal abuse, especially from a local councillor.

But then, I don't think he knew the councillor's granny.

Le Real McCoy

We went to Mazamet and were rather surprised to find the town up in arms. While *les Mazamétains* seemed quiet enough in themselves, there were posters and hoardings everywhere, neatly lettered and apparently professionally produced, proclaiming a deep municipal anger about something or other. *Mazamet en colère*, the posters raged: *Assez de paroles, assez de gestes.* Mazamet is furious: enough words, enough gestures. Clearly there was something wrong.

There was even *un barrage*, a favourite French demonstration device, on the N112, the main road, where they'd taken over the traffic lights and weren't letting anything through without making sure every driver was fully informed of the situation.

We didn't discover what it was. It goes against our British notions of freedom to be forcibly subjected to a political harangue or pamphleting campaign before being allowed to proceed, so we took a back way into the town. By the time we left it was gone midday, when everything in France, including outraged civic consciousness, discovers its appetite, and the traffic lights had taken over again.

Some days later I found myself spending 48 hours in a Toulouse hospital, the excellent Clinique Pasteur, for a minor operation.

Sharing my room the first evening was a compact, thick-set man of about 60. The matter of the moment wasn't a coronary artery *barrage'd* almost as effectively as the N112 had been in Mazamet (me), or the draining of a lung damaged by over-enthusiastic cycling up the Pyrenees (my companion), but a football match on television between Paris St Germain and Olympique Marseille.

Olympique Marseille is the team everyone loves to beat and, at that time, rarely did. OM, as it's popularly known, has survived match-fixing scandals, enormous fines, crippling demotions, in fact every sort of *barrage* to hinder their progress to the top of the French league. Home supporters bellow anti-OM chants whoever the opposition may be. Typically, the only train to break a regional railway strike that day was one carrying OM fans from Marseilles to Paris. Typically, the OM fans wrecked it.

But it wasn't OM's night. They lost 2-0, and from my companion's muted reaction I suspected that he might be an OM supporter and that I'd best tread a bit warily. I made one or two non-committal remarks to test the water, but I needn't have worried; my companion was passionately interested in football but wasn't much bothered who won as long as the game was good. Such even-handedness wasn't hard for him, he said. He wasn't actually French but Spanish. In fact he used to play for Real Madrid.

This was astounding. It was as though Billy Wright or Danny Blanchflower had suddenly surfaced in the next bed. Oh, but they were good days, my companion said, the late 50s and early 60s, when Real Madrid swept all before them. Yes, he'd played in Scotland. He'd been in Glasgow when they'd trounced Eintracht Frankfurt 7-3 to win the European Cup for the fifth time running. Glory days, when you knew you were safe with Puskas up front and Julio Iglesias in goal behind you.

'Julio Iglesias?' I asked. 'Do you mean the singer?'

'That's the one,' he said, 'but I knew him better as a footballer.'

This was another surprise. I knew that Vilem Tausky, at one time a popular conductor of extravaganza concerts in the Royal Albert Hall, had once kept goal for Czechoslovakia. Maybe there were certain psychological similarities between musicians and goalkeepers, making it easy to transfer from one to the other. And vice versa, of course. Fascinating.

In the morning, while he prepared for discharge and I for the surgeon's knife, there were other revelations. He'd been forced to retire from the game, because of a leg injury, at a time when there were few employment openings for him in Spain. A French friend had found him a job in Mazamet, where he'd lived ever since, running a haulage company in working hours and a cycling club in his spare time.

'Mazamet?' I said. 'The last time I was in Mazamet there was some kind of demonstration going on, road-blocks and that kind of thing. We never found out what it was all about.'

It turned out that my companion had been closely involved. The scourge of Mazamet was *les casseurs*, young people who steal cars, lash railway sleepers to them, drive into shop windows and loot the contents. Even in France . . . and because *les casseurs* usually come from an ethnic minority thought to be under-privileged, the police are sometimes slow to act for fear of provoking something worse, thus driving law-abiding *Mazamétains* to take matters into their own hands.

My companion spoke warmly about Mazamet vigilante groups, which he described as *une milice*, a militia. 'We'll show them,' he went on, with all the determination of one who'd stopped Pele and Beckenbauer in their tracks, to whom a few *casseurs* would be as gossamer before the gale. 'Why don't you join us? You'll see some fireworks!'

Just then the trolley arrived to cart me away to the operating table. Just as well, really. When I came back, he'd gone. I never did discover his name.

Her name was Annie, and she could have come from anywhere. She was about 20, neat, well-shod, dressed in the combat gear the young sometimes favour here, tidy hair, nails well trimmed, self-respect reasonably intact. She had a McDonald's waxed paper cup in front of her with a few coins in it, just enough to encourage you to put a few more in.

She was pretty, but to say she put the mimosa in the shade might be pushing it a bit, although the idea neatly links her with the first blossom of the year in the Languedoc. It's one of the first signs of returning spring, and there's often a race between it and the almond blossom to herald longer, sunnier days and thoughts of getting your *oignons* and *patates* in.

(*Patates*? What happened to *pommes de terre*? Yes, well, we discover as we penetrate the deeper strata of Midi rural life and letters that all French isn't as it's taught in school: *patates* is as acceptable as 'spuds' in England or 'tatties' in Scotland, all three terms with a down-to-earth flavour about them entirely suitable for potatoes. No, at the time of writing I hadn't got mine in, but I had dug in quantities of *fumier de cheval* which Claude Lauze delivered in French mailbags, ideal for the purpose, stoutly sewn and stencilled LA POSTE in bright yellow. Which brings me back to the mimosa.)

Our February landscape, still in its winter coat of drab browns and greens, is brilliantly patched with paint-box yellow where the mimosa trees have made it through the winter. Our own mini-copse is on a north-facing slope, so the masses of blossom burst out a day or two after their cousins in the sun across the valley. The scent is there already, a heady, musky fragrance that I find slightly sickly. So our blossom will stay where it is, unlike in many French homes where armfuls of it in big pots show that it's as popular as holly at Christmas.

Closely watching the mimosa blossom are the cohorts of Euro-unfortunates who appear to trudge round France and elsewhere following one flowering season after another, the Languedoc at mimosa-time, eastwards across the Rhone into Provence when the violets flower, over into Italy for the lily of the valley: a nameless, night-time people, surfacing briefly during the day to accost you in the streets of Béziers or Montpellier with a bunch of mimosa torn from somebody's garden and demanding a few *sous*. Some claim to speak no French at all, but thrust a grimy card at you explaining in excellent French that they're Kosovar, or Kurd, or Rwandan, or from whichever country is currently in the toils. It's terribly difficult not to be cynical about these people, as difficult as it is to take in that a country as wealthy as France finds it hard to come to terms with this problem.

But maybe Annie was different. She'd sold all her mimosa and had taken up her pitch in one of Montpellier's most lucrative sites, by the ticket machines in one of the city's wonders, the underground car-park beneath the magnificent traffic-free Place de la Comédie.

'*Bonjour,*' she said as I came down the steps, holding out her McDonald's cup and asking for some *pièces*. I had no change from the ticket machine, I was merely going down to the bowels of the earth to leave some shopping in the car. As I returned like Orpheus to the February sun a fellow mimosa-merchant was just taking his leave of her. 'OK, see you at 12.30,' she said, in the accents of fashionable Edinburgh, then, reverting to Euro-speak, '*ciao*'.

She was still there when we left Montpellier in the afternoon, still with a few coins in her cup. I hoped she hadn't had to learn the hard way that anything over a certain amount you cream off into your pocket and out of sight and temptation, leaving a small sum in your begging bowl as a pipe-opener. She was deep in conversation with another girl about the operation of a mobile phone. In German.

Who was this Scots girl, with at least three languages under her belt, begging her way round Montpellier, selling hooky mimosa? I grieved for a Europe that could allow such things to happen, that could allow such talent to waste. But maybe things aren't always what they seem? At 18 I too was a Euro-down-and-out, absolutely by my own choice, doing the Grand Tour by rule of thumb, that's to say by waving it at traffic going in the direction I wanted to go. There wasn't any mimosa on the road to Vienna, as far as I remember, but perhaps Annie's future isn't so bleak. Perhaps she too could end up as a columnist with a weekly Scottish newspaper. *Ciao*.

Drainspotting

There it was in the letter-box, a slip of paper I couldn't ignore. 'Maître Zany', it said, and it seemed that he valued our potential custom so highly that he'd come all the way from Béziers to slip his calling card into our letter-box. You don't have to take all that seriously anyone styling themselves *maître*, master, a splendidly Renaissance title, but all the same it's how lawyers address each other. And musicians too: we say *maestro* – the same word – in English and even I as the conductor of a small choir have been called *maître* by respectable musicians. Not always easy to live up to.

'Maître Zany', the card read, and it soon became obvious that although he was neither lawyer nor musician his mastery of capital letters was beyond dispute: 'Famous MEDIUM, SEER and HEALER, renowned for his Wide Experience and Competence, Resolves all your Problems, Realises your Projects and Desires, even the most Desperate Cases: Return of your Loved One on the Exact Date . . .'

I enjoyed translating all this until I came up against a word I'd never seen before: *Désenvoûtement*. I was really stuck. *Voûte* meant vault, I knew. Something to do with taking out of the vault? Disenvaultment? The recovery of buried things, the finding of missing

73

persons or property? Treasure, even? For once the faithful, well-thumbed 2-volume 1938 Harrap French-English dictionary that I once disenvaulted from a jumble sale let me down. No mention of it. Never mind. It's wonderful what you can do with intelligent guesswork.

Maître Zany finished his spiel by offering to cure all Physical and Moral Complexes with Work that was 100% GUARANTEED, and promised results in 3 days.

A day or two after this calling card had enlivened a coffee break the drains started playing up. The bath wouldn't run away, the loos . . . but I don't need to go into detail. M. Belloc the plumber had to be sent for. His first question was terse and to the point: *La fosse, où elle est?* Now it doesn't take very long, living in France, to realise that French as she is spoke isn't always as she is taught, and if M. Belloc had been to a respectable Scottish school he would have said *où est la fosse septique?* But we're as used to colloquial French now as we are to the bizarre French notion that a septic tank is feminine, and the chief point of this linguistic blether is to put off the shameful admission that when it came to the exact location of the septic tank, we didn't know. Nobody knew, in fact. *Un mystère.*

'*Mercredi!*' M. Belloc said, which means Wednesday, using a plumber's euphemism for what you might normally find in the septic tank if you're lucky enough to know where yours is. He clearly wasn't going to spend his entire Wednesday or any other day probing for a missing septic tank, so he stuck a high-pressure hose, called *un karcher* here, down a suitable trap, squeezed the trigger and presently a sort of gurgling sneeze sounded the All Clear.

Hélas! It turned out only the next day that M. Belloc's *karcher* had been about as effective as a noseblow is in curing a cold. Back to square one. Truly a Desperate Case. Long, agonised discussions followed, pipe, magnifying glass and deerstalker stuff worthy of the detective the French call Sharlockoms; where could the septic tank be? The ante was upped, the big guns called up in the form of Christian

Cabrol the builder and his son Fabien, prop forward of a rugby club in the curiously-named Minervois village of Homps.

There were strange looks on receiving the request to *désenvoûter la fosse septique, s'il vous plaît,* but a few minutes' drilling through the concrete outside the front door brought cries of *Ah! la voilà!* There she is! And there she was indeed, our long-lost septic tank, still as feminine as she was on the day when she was buried in concrete more than 25 years ago.

The light dawned: 25 years, too, since she was last emptied. Fabien showed the true courage of a Homps front row forward and drew back her cover . . . let it be enough to say that if there isn't a branch of archaeology which deals with the contents of septic tanks, then there ought to be.

You may of course be wondering why Maître Zany wasn't called in. Surely with his Wide Experience and Competence finding an errant septic tank would have been child's play? A glance in his crystal ball, a quick shuffle of the Tarot cards? Well, perhaps, but you see I couldn't look him in the eye; *désenvoûtement,* I found in the spanking new Harraps CDRom French-English dictionary I got to replace the 1938 vintage, has nothing to do with recovery of buried things, treasure trove or lost property. I guessed wrong. It means Lifting a Spell or Curse.

Although, maybe, on second thoughts . . .

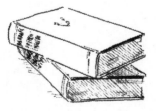

PLACES

Renaissance Journey

'You have acted like gods,' the warm-up man insisted, with a bravura gesture before the black curtain. 'In fact, you are gods!' His audience of about 30 would surely have bristled appreciatively, if the deafening bang that followed this apotheosis hadn't momentarily incapacitated them. An unusual proposition, to say the least; it's not every day that someone clothes you with notions of divinity, indeed blasts them into you.

But then it's not every day that the French national consciousness focuses on historic France: once a year only, when *Les Journées du Patrimoine*, Heritage Days, take up a mid-September weekend. It's an end-of-season time when the French take time off from counting the foreign tourist shekels tumbling in from the great sites like Mont St Michel, Rocamadour or Carcassonne, and enjoy their own, like the hosts polishing off the remaining goodies after the supper guests have gone. It's a time when, free of charge or at very reduced prices, you can choose from a huge range of museums, galleries, *châteaux* and historic sites.

We chose a whole town. Hearing that Pézenas featured in the local *Journées du Patrimoine* programme, we set off there one Sunday, trading our Haut Languedoc foothills for the Bas Languedoc plain, exchanging our wooded slopes and hairpin bends for the broad highways and the sky-wide vineyards, almost ready for harvesting, of the coastal plain. Pézenas is a town of about 8000 people who call themselves *les Piscénois* after the Roman name for the town, Piscenae. It has an unexpected link with the UK: on the approaches to the town, among the light industrial estates and pepperpot scatterings of new villas, there are signs reading PEZENAS *jumelée avec* MARKET DRAYTON. One man lies at the origin of this Hérault-Shropshire twinning: Robert Clive, Clive of India, the thorn in the side of the French expansionists when Britain and France were squabbling for the upper hand in India in the 1750s. Having done what he could to make sure the map of India would be coloured red for the next two centuries, Lord Clive returned home to his native Market Drayton with a retinue of Indian servants and his pockets stuffed with rupees. He broke his journey at Pézenas, where he stayed for some time at the nearby Château de Larzac. That he was able to stay there at all says a great deal for the comparatively civilised 18th-century manner of conducting wars. A less enlightened age would probably have lynched him.

However, Robert Clive wasn't the first celebrity to visit Pézenas, the financial and political capital of the Languedoc before Montpellier eclipsed it in the late 17th-century as the principal city of the area. The provincial *parlement* met here under the presidency of the princely families of Montmorency and Conti, and its sophistication and cultural reputation drew the great French dramatist Molière to work here.

Three centuries and more later, it's again a lively and prosperous little town, its elegant Renaissance heritage reclaimed from the worst ravages of time, sulphur dioxide and Coca-Cola ads, its past preserved while still being a comfortable place to live in.

We parked in the Place du 14 Juillet and followed signs to the start of guided tours of the Old Quarter, due to leave every 30 minutes from the Place Gambetta, where waiting groups were warmed up. A huge black curtain sealed off the starting street, turning the tour into a kind of theatre; appropriately enough, given the connection of Pézenas with Molière and the fact that the guides were drama students from the local colleges.

The warmer-up welcomed us. 'Welcomed' is too tepid: he seethed and drooled with enthusiasm for our presence. '*Braves gens, que vous êtes merveilleux* . . . good people, how wonderful you are! You have done everything asked of you, you have done it so well, with such style! You have heard of Pézenas, you have located Pézenas, you have come to Pézenas, you have arrived on exactly the right day, at precisely the right time! How irreproachable your sense of direction! How impeccable your sense of timing!'

All this was rather rudely interrupted at intervals by his assistant shouting out *trois minutes . . . deux minutes . . . une minute*, driving the warmer-up onwards to his furious climax: 'You have played your parts like celestial beings, you have acted like gods; in fact, you are gods!' At this cue there was a shattering explosion from a maroon detonated somewhere behind the curtain, startled pigeons fluttered about ornate Renaissance cornices, small children cried, dogs barked, the black curtain was swept back and the tour started.

We were shepherded from patch to patch by drama-student guides. Some found the warm-up a difficult act to follow and rambled on about who built what and when. But others, who would surely be awarded 'A's for their drama practicals, sparkled with lively stories and a real enthusiasm for their patch. There's an art in bringing Renaissance mullions or architraves to life for the passing *Journées du Patrimoine* crowd, and some of these young people had it in full measure. Molière would have signed them up without a second thought.

The organisers had worked hard, and not just with the splendid Pézenas architecture. In the entrance courtyard of the Hôtel de Lacoste – not a hotel but a fine town house – someone was playing a viola da gamba, ancestor of the 'cello, sending curlicues of Baroque quavers up the handsome balustraded stairwell. At the Porte du Ghetto we suddenly found ourselves involved in street theatre as three members from the local drama club argued whether Molière had really worked in Pézenas, or whether it was just an Office du Tourisme myth. Just as they were about to settle it with their fists, a figure with quill and parchment, dressed in fashionable 17th-century costume, emerged from a nearby shoe shop, silencing the arguing trio as he crossed the street, tapping his temple, winking at the audience and finally disappearing into a *pâtisserie*. Fascinating. Inventive, too.

We drove home feeling that we would like to return to Pézenas, and soon, and explore it at our own pace, which was probably the point of the *Journées du Patrimoine* exercise. Our only souvenir was a local speciality, some miniature stove-pipe pastries called *petits pâtés de Pézenas*. There was a distinctly Indian flavour to them: the filling inside the little pastry cylinder was of lamb sweetened with brown sugar, curry and candied lemon peel. An acquired taste. Maybe Lord Clive taught *les Piscénois* to acquire it.

Vintage Minervois

There's a local saying to the effect that everyone learns by their mistakes, even God: after he had created Provence, he made the Minervois. Not much of a comparison, really. A bit cheeky, too, like saying after he'd made Copacabana Beach he made Clacton. All the same, the Minervois is very special: a private, almost unknown land of low, rolling hills with rocky outcrops, pencil-slim cypress trees, olives, almonds and endless patchworks of vineyards between ancient sun-bleached villages.

It's forty minutes away to the south from our valley, a sort of buffer state between the Languedoc hills and the sea. The road from Bardou winds up through dense woods, and when the crest is reached, the watershed between Mediterranean and Atlantic France, a surprising thing happens: the vegetation changes completely, within a couple of kilometres. Instead of cowslips and hellebore and forests of green and sun-stippled – in high summer, at least – beech and chestnut, the hills are clothed in impenetrable sweeps of *chêne vert*, evergreen Mediterranean oak. Harsh stony upland expanses of *garrigue* are dotted with dwarf juniper, cistus and wild thyme. The road drops, and on the horizon there's a burnished streak, bright in the morning sun: the Mediterranean. The *garrigue* slowly gives way to vines, planted in their neat rows, and you're in the Minervois.

It's called Minervois after Minerve, a village of about 100 souls – more in high summer, but fewer in winter when the holiday houses are closed up and blind with their shutters fastened – which features on most visitors' lists of places to see. From a distance it looks like any other village in the area, a cluster of ochre tiles and stone walls bleached to a leathery greyness by centuries of sun. Close to, it becomes an eyrie, a fortress, perched precariously on a tongue of cliff where two gorges meet. It looks as if a strong wind, or even a gentle push, would send it all tumbling into the ravine.

Somebody else thought so a long time ago. As you stand on the opposite clifftop you notice, a little distance away on the edge of a vineyard, a large wooden contraption that defies any apparent purpose. An enormous climbing frame? A drilling rig? Suddenly, perhaps with a gasp, you realise what it is: it's a huge catapult, one of those extraordinary engines of war that hurled boulders at the walls of mediaeval castles or lobbed vats of Greek fire into Saracen-held Jerusalem. What on earth is it doing here?

In fact it's a replica of a catapult nicknamed La Malvoisine, the bad neighbour, by those on the receiving end, a replica put there by someone who cares enough about Minerve's past to commemorate certain events in 1210, when the village wouldn't have been a very comfortable place in which to live. The Languedoc, not then incorporated into France proper, was in the grip of a crusade to exterminate the Cathars, a sect that refused to acknowledge the Pope's authority and which, perhaps more importantly, occupied rich lands controlling the strategic routes into and out of Spain.

Troops moved in, led on behalf of the French king, Philippe-Auguste, and Pope Innocent III by Simon de Montfort, grandfather of the man who founded the first English parliament fifty years later. The city of Béziers fell after a bitter struggle, and according to the chroniclers all the inhabitants, Cathar and Catholic alike, were slaughtered. A soldier anxious to spare Catholics asked the papal legate Arnaud Amaury how he might distinguish them. 'Kill them all,' Amaury replied. 'God will recognise his own.'

Carcassonne and Narbonne fell, leaving isolated pockets of resistance for Simon de Montfort's troops to mop up. Minerve was one, apparently secure on its clifftop and protected by a fortress of which only one tower now remains. The Cathars held out through the long, hot summer months of 1210 until bombardment by La Malvoisine smashed the last well and the inhabitants were parched into surrender. Given the choice between conversion or death, 140 Cathars chose the flames. The Place des Martyrs commemorates them.

At one time, beguiled by the sun and the summer swallows, we briefly considered buying a house in Minerve. It was a fascinating place, at the end of the rue du Caïre, Cairo Street. A narrow donkey-wide lane, it petered out into a footpath leading down to the site of the last well, le Puits St Rustique, and past a pen where the neighbours kept a couple of wild boar, endlessly digging for freedom.

The floor of one downstairs room was entirely covered with drying almonds, and the garden ended abruptly at the cliff edge, so handy, as generations of Minervois must have found, for weeds and garden rubbish. But for all the sun and summer swallows there was the same air of sadness that you find at Culloden Moor, or certain areas of Flanders, or any other killing field where man's inhumanity to man has left its forlorn vestiges. Besides, Minerve hums with tourists in summer.

So we didn't buy the house, instead making ourselves very comfortably at home with another local product: quality Minervois wines rival their claret cousins from further west. Why buy the house when you can drink the wine?

Joust A Minute

Sorry about the title. There's no excuse, really. It comes of spending half a lifetime in primary schools. Bear it in mind, though; it's sure to come in useful later on.

Today's destination is the town of Agde. Unusually for the bubbling, chattering French they speak in the Midi, the bane of those who have slaved to get their tongues round school or evening-class French, you don't pronounce the last letter, which grammarians will recognise as a mute *e*. Agg'd. There. Spoken like a true *Agathois*.

There aren't many towns older than Agde along France's Mediterranean coast. Nearly 2500 years ago Greek colonists, hugging the coast as they did, suddenly found themselves rounding a headland and pulling against the offshore freshwater currents at the estuary of the river Hérault.

The river washed the foot of an easily defensible site, an outcrop of black basalt quite unusual along this coast. 'Good,' they said, in Greek, and if you're called Agatha you'll know it means 'good', although I don't expect you've been about so long that your name has been time-worn into Agde. The original Greek lingers on in the local adjective *agathois*, coming from Agde.

There isn't much the Greek founders, the original *Agathois*, would recognise today. The coastline has changed, the old town is now a kilometre or two inland, and acres of holiday apartments, marinas and campsites, called Cap d'Agde to distinguish them from the old town, now sprawl over the reclaimed river-borne silts, salt-marshes and longshore drifting of the endless Mediterranean sands. Wait, though: the early Greeks might just catch an echo in the name Heliopolis, Sun City, Europe's largest nudist colony, whose denizens – to continue the Greek idiom, where 'denizen' means 'occupant' or 'dweller' – whose denizens, mainly Dutch, it seems, surrender themselves to total sun-worship on the sands and among the dunes.

However, the draw to Agde wasn't an urge to go Dutch but a concert to be given by a Viennese string quartet, the Goldberg Ensemble, in the cathedral. Klaus Erhardt, a cultivated German sheep-farmer and concert promoter (who has made it a fascinating lifetime's work to restore the other Bardou in the area, virtually a total ruin on the upper slopes of Mt Caroux when he bought it), had urged us to go to swell the numbers. They threatened to be pitifully small because the Agde *Office des Arts et de la Culture* had omitted to publicise it. No announcement in the local press, no posters, nothing.

There were other doom-factors, too. We were paying for days of endless sun and temperatures well into the 90s, with violent thunderstorms and sudden cloudbursts all afternoon, quite enough to deter any local chamber music-lovers who might happen to be hanging about by the cathedral door that evening. Worse, there was extraordinary activity, between the showers, just across the river Hérault from the cathedral. Bursts of *fortissimo* trumpet fanfares and deafening, unintelligible announcements from an *Agathois* commentator joyfully seizing on every mute *e* in the vocabulary boomed out over the water from massive speakers fixed to riverside trees. If this was to last into the evening, it boded ill for any string quartet spinning out the delicate gossamer of a Schubert *pianissimo*.

But there was an hour to kill before the concert started. A waterside restaurant beckoned insistently, and beneath the striped awning of Le Terrisse all thought of the string quartet vanished for the moment, swept away by the prospect of the local fish soup and *le spectacle* across the river, maybe 50 metres wide at that point.

Soupe de poisson in this part of the world is a bit of *un spectacle* too. There's much more to it than conveying a laden spoon to the mouth. It comes in a mini-tureen, and all the fish will have been passed through a sieve to remove any bones and fins. It's served with toasted slices of *baguette*, which you spread with *rouille*, a sort of spicy fish mayonnaise, and sprinkle with finely grated cheese. You then launch your rafts of toast one by one into your soup, where they sink slowly and the cheese melts. It's perfectly delicious . . .

. . . and speaking of launching, across the river beneath the raucous loudspeakers two boats, one blue, one red, were in the water, each crewed by half-a-dozen firemen in navy blue shorts and white T-shirts.

Each boat had a stepped ramp at the stern, on which a fireman perched, armed like a sort of mediaeval water-knight with a long lance and a shield. The boats drew apart, turned to face each other, a trumpet fanfare announced the first round, the outboard motors roared, the boats closed fast. The jousters levelled their lances, and a huge cheer went up from the crowds now gathered on the banks as the red fireman knocked the blue fireman into the water, to be picked up by a rescue dinghy. I don't think the crowd would have minded much who fell in the water, as long as someone did, but after about a dozen rounds the last blue jouster knocked the last red off his perch, so the blue team had won. They actually use the word joust too, only in its French form *joute*. Next week, the commentator promised us, two teams of policemen would compete in *les joutes*. Customs officers, waiters and trade union officials were lined up in the coming weeks. We were rather disappointed that the denizens of Heliopolis hadn't entered a team.

The thunder, trumpets, splashes, shouts and cheers were all over by the time the concert started. The audience numbered just 16 and the Goldberg Ensemble played like demigods, even unto the delicate gossamer of their Schubert *pianissimi*. Klaus, a German, asked me, a Brit, to announce in French the programme to be given by some Austrian musicians in an ancient Greek colony. That's Europe for you.

Breakout From Béziers

'*Ça va les décourager*,' the taxi driver said cheerfully. 'That'll cool the tourists' ardour. That'll send them packing home. Nothing like a good thunderstorm to see them off. If the first doesn't, the second will. They'll soon vanish, you'll see.'

Taxi drivers, like barbers, are founts of assured wisdom the world over, probably because they're in a position to practise and perfect their observations and one-liners over and over again, each time with new customers. I've forgotten his name, but he wore the universal uniform of Béziers taxi drivers, flip-flops, wash-faded shorts, Chinese-produced T-shirt with an incomprehensible slogan in English: US VITAMIN SURFER.

Anyway, we were glad to see him, because the car had broken down.

To pinpoint the exact spot where we stood forlorn and wheel-less, we start with the city of Béziers, a white and dusty cathedral town whose ancient bastions stand on a bluff above the river Orb like a single tooth. City traffic in summer is dreadful, a perpetual battle for position round the city's proudest feature, the Allées Paul Riquet, a magnificent pedestrian avenue lined with plane trees, stretching from the Theatre almost down to the Jardin des Poètes, a park commemorating by day the many poets who have written in Languedocien, the most local of the six or seven Occitan dialects, and by night, apparently, harbouring Béziers' less fortunate social stratum. Paul Riquet, incidentally, was the 17th-century engineer who conceived and designed the Canal du Midi, a successful attempt to link the Atlantic with the Mediterranean, thus avoiding the necessity of sailing all the way round Spain and Portugal. One of the Béziers bridges carries his canal, now mainly used for pleasure craft, across the river.

The Allées are something like the Spanish *rambla*, a large shady open space in the centre of the town, and indeed the Spanish element is strong in Béziers: the great annual festival is the *feria*, which revolves round bullfighting, a Philistine if full-blooded and flamboyant spectacle which attracts as many tourists as it repels but which seems close to the hearts of the *Biterrois*, the people of Béziers. Personally, and I expect predictably, I would rather have my teeth pulled than take my seat in the *arènes*, an enormous circular bull-ring a little way from the town centre, modelled on the Coliseum in Rome, to witness a depraved barbarity that passes for theatre . . .

. . . or even be condemned for ever to swirl in the traffic round the periphery of the Allées Paul Riquet. It wouldn't surprise me to learn that the Béziers municipal police occasionally gather up the bleached skeletons of foreign tourists, bony fingers still clamped to the steering wheels of camper vans ineluctably swept on by the press of traffic, their ragged T-shirts reading NO ESCAPE FROM THE CENTRE LANE. Charlton Heston had an easier time of it in the famous chariot race in *Ben Hur*.

However, this wasn't our problem. Béziers is fringed with extensive Zones d'Activités Commerciales, shortened to ZAC, and here you'll find all the major French retail chains, Géant and Auchan hypermarkets, Lapeyre reach-me-down joinery, Decathlon sports goods and so on: all the signs that despite the apparent poverty and rural backwardness of the Languedoc the economic pulse of consumerist France beats fast enough.

But in the car park attached to Darty, a nationwide chain of electrical stores, the Midi sun beat down pitilessly on a lifeless car, immobilised in the torrid heat by a flat battery. Hence the taxi, summoned thanks to the helpful staff at Darty and Europ Assistance, who arranged to have the car towed away. It was during the taxi-ride home that the driver shared with us his feelings about tourists, whom he referred to as *estivants*, summer-ers. And about thunderstorms.

There'd been a cracker that morning, the first of the storms we get towards the end of every August. After numberless days, weeks, of cloudless skies and high temperatures, the storm broke. It lasted for 4 hours, rolling round and round our valley as though imprisoned by the mountains like *estivants* trying to escape from the Allées Paul Riquet merry-go-round.

Torrents, cascades of rain ravaged the fig tree on the *terrasse* and sent a promising purple crop tumbling and pulping into the lane below. Mighty buffets of wind tore at the shutters straining uneasily at their fasteners and we had a cold breakfast by candlelight: the first casualty is always the electricity. It went on for so long that Bellamy the golden retriever, usually a quivering, slavering wreck at the first distant roll of thunder, lay down and slept while the skies split and the elements slugged it out. Eventually it rolled on, or wore itself out, and the sun took over again in the early afternoon when we headed south for Béziers.

In *A Year in Provence* Peter Mayle stresses, quite rightly, the full-bloodedness and flamboyance of the Midi, the light, the colour, the wine, the noise, the scents, the growth, the way food tastes, and he could have added the thunderstorms and, for that matter, the Béziers traffic. All too heady for Northerners, he decides, who can only take so much of it at once. So the storm-triggered annual trek north starts, snail-like Dutch caravans in beaming ignorance of the immense queue of impatient taxi drivers trying to overtake them, German camper vans bristling with mountain bikes, sailboards and pushchairs testifying to their various holiday activities, bronzed Swedes hanging their limbs out of car windows with a freedom I suppose they can't normally enjoy in Stockholm, the odd Wallace and Gromit-like Brit, storm-soaked tent stuffed into the sidecar.

Another storm or two and the French should get their Mediterranean beaches to themselves for a few sunny September weeks. The tourist-free Allées Paul Riquet will be easier to navigate, too, and maybe our taxi driver will find a T-shirt that says ABOUT FACE LEMMINGS, but I don't expect he'll be any the wiser.

The car was back on the road almost immediately, incidentally. They really get on with it, French mechanics. Even during thunderstorms.

Rennes Le Château Revisited

Finding Rennes le Château, while on holiday in France back in 1982, wasn't easy. There weren't any signposts. Apparently the locals had removed them; tourists weren't welcome. The map located it somewhere slightly to the east of the main road that runs south along the valley of the river Aude from Carcassonne, and after a lot of to-ing and fro-ing in the village of Couiza we found a narrow country road winding sharply upwards, climbing about 300 metres in about 3 kilometres – nothing exceptional, because the area is humped and ridged with rocky hills – and there we were: Rennes le Château at last. It didn't seem anything very special. Was this really the place that had launched a thousand best-sellers?

Barely 25 people can have lived there. The *château*, a mediaeval fortress, looked as though one glancing blow from La Malvoisine, somehow transported from Minerve, would have reduced it to a dusty heap of stones and wormy roof-timbers, and with one exception the houses were the usual Midi cheek-by-jowl jumble of stone-built, orange-tiled village dwellings. The exception was a handsome villa with dormer windows, facing an untidy formal garden with low box hedges and a waterless fountain in the middle of a dry *bassin*. Perched on the edge of a cliff at the top of the hill was an unusual neo-Gothic circular tower of dressed stone, with a spectacular view over the surrounding countryside. A decrepit conservatory and aviary – if aviary it was; it might just as well have been a monkey-house – peeped out from an overgrown garden, a jungle, which linked the tower with the gabled villa. No one lived there now, that was certain. Somebody of some means might once have done.

Surprisingly, the church was open. It wasn't much different from many Midi country churches, garishly decorated by our northern standards: plaster saints with eyes that followed you about and all kinds of full-blooded imagery to remind the faithful of their place and purpose on earth – and eventually either above it or, more likely, below . . . it wasn't a comfortable place. We were glad to leave.

(We weren't the only ones to feel uncomfortable: years later I compared notes with friends who'd found their way, independently, to Rennes le Château in the 70s. They'd asked several apparently innocent questions about the Cathars. They'd received short shrift and stones were thrown at their car as they left. Clearly visitors were discouraged, maybe not without reason, because not long before a treasure hunter had dynamited an old well, convinced that the Lost Treasure of Jerusalem lay at the bottom. The resulting shower of rocks and débris smashed many village roof tiles.)

It was a book that drew us there. We would never have heard of Rennes le Château if it hadn't featured in a best-seller called *The Holy Blood and The Holy Grail*, co-written by Henry Lincoln, Richard Leigh and Michael Baigent. We were fascinated by its revelations: in the closing years of the 19th-century the village priest, Bérenger Saunière, discovered something, perhaps connected with the Knights Templar, that made him fabulously wealthy. He found coded parchments hinting at a Grand Secret which would rock empires and dynasties; he spent hours digging and fossicking in his church, alone unless his housekeeper Marie Denarnaud held his lantern. He made unexplained trips to Paris, he became a friend of Claude Debussy, he shocked his colleagues with his revelations. In 1916 – when France and Austria-Hungary, as it then was, were at war – the Viennese Emperor's brother, Archduke Johann, came to see him secretly.

He lavished extraordinary and costly decoration on his church. He built himself a palatial presbytery, with a cliff-top tower a short distance away. His gardens included a conservatory and a modest zoo. He died in 1917, having foretold his own death to the day. Marie Denarnaud, who inherited his wealth and his secret, survived until 1953, taking what she knew to the grave.

All this first broke in France in 1956, when a regional newspaper, *La Dépêche du Midi*, ran the story in several successive issues. An amiable fantasist called Gérard de Sède turned it into a book, *L'Or de Rennes*, The Gold of Rennes. In Britain it was picked up in due course by Henry Lincoln, a writer with esoteric leanings, who was partly responsible for three BBC 'Chronicle' programmes which scratched the surface of the Rennes le Château story and Saunière's secret.

The Holy Blood and The Holy Grail explored the mystery further and quickly became a best-seller. It came to a sensational conclusion: there is a wealthy secret society dedicated to the preservation and eventual reinstatement of Jesus' lineal descendants, who were alive and well and living in Paris. The Rennes le Château connection was almost incidental: in mediaeval times this obscure village in the Pyrenean foothills was the fortified treasury of the secret society. Saunière discovered pointers to the Grand Secret and some of the treasure, hidden when the society, strongly connected with the Knights Templar, was almost exterminated by the French king Philippe le Bel, whose real motivation was to lay his hands on their reputedly fabulous wealth. The whole story is a wonderful farrago of shadowy secret societies, hidden treasure and mysterious coded parchments. Saunière is supposed to have decorated his church like a gigantic crossword clue, in such a way as to show where the remaining treasure lies hidden, in caves or underground chambers around the village.

Another best-seller, issued from a similar stable, *The Tomb of God*, suggested that Jesus was finally buried under a nearby mountain. Huge quantities of ink, midnight oil, paper and computer memory have been lavished on the Rennes le Château mystery. (This just adds to it, of course.) Everything is grist to the mystery mill, the Book of Revelations, the Arthurian cycle, the Cathars, the Knights Templar, the Great Pyramid, UFOs, the Rosicrucians, Freemasons, Atlantis, Nostradamus, Old Moore's Almanac and *The Hobbit*, I shouldn't be surprised.

We went back to Rennes le Château one Christmas, 14 years after our first visit, 14 years which had seen a cosy little mystery turn into an industry. The village itself seemed unscathed: little had changed. A car with a UK number plate stood outside a house undergoing renovations, and we wondered if someone else had become as hooked from afar as we'd been. A little shop sold ice-lollies, souvenirs, cards and copies of *l'Enigme Sacré*, the French version of *The Holy Blood and The Holy Grail*. The dormer-windowed villa, in fact Saunière's presbytery, had been turned into a modest museum, with one or two pictures, some vestments and furniture, nothing very interesting. The church was locked. A handwritten notice pinned to the door advertised Midnight Mass at 6.30 on Christmas Eve. We remembered Abbé Pic at Les Verreries de Moussans, and the demands made on him by surrounding congregations for Midnight Masses: Rennes le Château can no longer have had its own *curé*. Times had changed.

* * *

After a cathedral concert one July evening, I was sitting with Abbé Quatrefages, the St Pons *archiprêtre* and a well-known church archaeologist, on the *terrasse* of the Bar du Palais. I mentioned Rennes le Château. '*Oui,*' he said, laughing. '*Je sais tout.* I know everything.' He explained Saunière's wealth: quite accidentally, he had discovered two or three tombs underneath his church while workmen were in the process of replacing the old altar, which, set into the end wall of the church, had become unsafe. They contained grave goods, a few jewels, a small gold chalice of no great antiquity. He gave most away to his colleagues and to his housekeeper and her family, whose descendants still have them. There was no treasure, no fortune. Nor were there any parchments, which no one has ever seen anyway. The hollow pillar in which the legend-merchants claim he found them is rock solid. Kaiser Franz-Josef had no brother Johann. No secrets, either, about the decoration of his church. Most of the items came from church suppliers' catalogues and can be found throughout France.

But Saunière did have his own secret: he traded in saying private Masses, advertising his services throughout France and abroad, far beyond the official limit of three per day. His fees amounted to many thousands of francs, representing so many Masses that he never caught up with a huge backlog. He was called to account by the Bishop of Carcassonne and suspended, but by that time his church had been restored and the presbytery and tower built, although not fully paid for. At his death he left some unpaid contractors' bills. His housekeeper had to sell the grave-jewels he'd given her to pay them off.

So far, so prosaic. Maybe I shouldn't have mentioned Rennes le Château to Abbé Quatrefages. It's best not to prick the bubbles of romance: we need a dressing of distant dreams to ginger up our daily diet. Maybe they're best left as they are: a mystery explained isn't a mystery any longer, but a reminder of the tricks your judgement gets up to the moment you take your eye off it.

'And the Grand Secret?' I asked. Abbé Quatrefages just smiled. But then he would, wouldn't he?

Up and up the road led us, until it seemed as though down wasn't a direction that existed any more, and that what the car's dashboard really needed was an altimeter. Pine forest gave way to bare rock and scree, mountain streams chattered and tumbled at the foot of precipices we tried to pretend weren't there, the railway that had accompanied us up the valley disappeared into a tunnel. A final stiff climb and we arrived in Andorra, after a four-hour journey into the heart of the Pyrenees: an awkward, switchback journey, valley-hopping over the douce hills of the Minervois to Carcassonne and the river Aude, then over a prettily Alpine spur of Pyrenean foothills to the valley of the Ariège, and finally a climb of 2000 metres among the midsummer snow patches and the jags and needles of the high tops to Pas de la Case, one of the very few passes across one of the great mountain barriers of history.

I don't remember any demands to get out of the car to kiss the sacred soil of Andorra or otherwise mark our arrival in a new country. The reports we'd heard of Andorra, from friends and neighbours who'd been on bus trips organised for some reason by the Labastide fire brigade, weren't particularly encouraging. Good for shopping and skiing, but otherwise thumbs down for a grey, uninteresting place, whose monosyllabic place-names – Llorts, Pal, Prats, Ertz – don't have too much bubbling *joie de vivre* about them, although maybe the polysyllabic ski resorts – Soldeu, Arinsal – suggest a bit more of a *frisson* of sophistication.

There was a time when as a green and callow youth I'd enjoyed collecting stamps on my passport, even going to the length of asking the more amiable frontier officials for them. The biggest and most elaborate, worth a dozen measly Boulognes or Ostends, came from the rubber stamp of one of Europe's tiniest countries, relics of a

Ruritanian order of social organisation, and one moreover that it had just taken me a little over an hour to walk across en route from Austria to Switzerland: Fuerstentum Liechtenstein, it read, next to the Count of Liechtenstein's coat of arms. This jejune passion for passport stamps disappeared long before I'd got the length of other mini-states, Monaco, Luxembourg, the Vatican or San Marino – or Andorra.

It could have resurfaced in Andorra. There were frontier guards amiable enough at Pas de la Case, splendid in pink shirts and pale blue tunics, as though they'd been recruited from some operetta like *The Gipsy Baron* or *The Chocolate Soldier* or, if it comes to that, *The Count of Liechtenstein*. But frontier guards were a reminder that Andorra, a tiny independent state about the size of Nairnshire or Rutland, isn't a member state of the European Union, and they've surely been taught to smile at the thousands of French and other visitors pouring daily over the pass in search of tax-free goodies. You can buy almost anything under the sun here, free of VAT, purchase tax, sales tax, import duty, whatever. So we went unashamedly in search of bargains.

Andorra tilts down towards Spain, a bowl of a few steep-sided valleys reaching back to the Pyrenean crests. At Pas de la Case everything French suddenly stops, including the language. It's easier to get by in English than in French, and even Spanish is a distant cousin of the local language, Catalan, a tongue that sounds like a faulty fuse-box with all its shushing, clicking and hissing. Pas de la Case confirms your suspicions that Andorra is really one gigantic tax-free supermarket in the middle of nowhere. It's like puffing up to the middle of Exmoor and finding all the shopping centres you've ever been in dumped there. Because the Andorran valleys are so steep-to, the buildings are tall, jostling together shoulder to shoulder in a wild clash of architectural styles. Not a pretty sight. No one went to Andorra for its loveliness.

Our first stop, some way down the road from Pas de la Case, was a four-storey jerry-built shack called Comerç Espunyes. A momentary light dawned: *comerç* must surely be the same word as *commerce*? – but philology took a back seat among the tons of ceramics, garden statuary, alabaster lamps, bronze figurines . . . and booze, barrels and barrels of it, ranged on shelves round a dank and ill-lit showroom and labelled in a spidery hand *Porto, Pastis, Coniac, Xnaps* and many more. An elderly, shambling man, maybe Señor Espunyes himself, shuffled in, handed out plastic 2-litre mini-barrels and indicated that we could sample whatever we liked: there were minute glass tankards slung on a wire beside each barrel.

The first barrel had *wiski* scrawled on it. I opened the tap and had a quick micro-snifter, enough to confirm that the licensed trade in Scotland had little to fear from Señor Espunyes' *wiski*, even though his price for 2 litres would barely have covered the customary fifth of a gill served north of the Border. His 'Cointreau' was a pleasant surprise, though, and we went away with our mini-barrel, noticing as we left a large shed over the road suspiciously labelled *distilleria*.

We stopped again further down the main valley, where the shop-fronts and showrooms become continuous for a dozen or so kilometres and where a stranger only knows he's crossed a local boundary by the changing police uniforms, operatic again in their many-coloured splendour. Necessary, too, to control the swarms of huge 4-wheel drives with which the Andorrans clutter up their tiny country.

We bought a cordless phone, a fax-cum-answering machine and a new mixer-blender, all much cheaper than in France. Then home, and a burning question: should we return the way we came, or follow the valley down into Spain and slip back into France through the side door? Either way, Doomsday might await, in the form of the Customs. We thought a French number plate would draw less attention crossing into Spain, so we turned south.

We were quite wrong. A less than amiable Spanish Customs officer waved us into a vacant inspection bay and told me to open the boot. Despair. There it lurked, our contraband, sniggering, as though it was a cigarette packet discovered inconveniently close to me behind the bike sheds at playtime. But he barely glanced at it. '*C'est bon*,' he said, assuming we were French, and turned to the next car. We sped off as though we'd been given extra playtime. I don't know what he was looking for. Señor Espunyes' *wiski*, maybe.

Back home, I found the fax operating instructions were in Spanish, a language I stagger about in uncertainly. I couldn't even fax M. Gonzalez to ask him to come and translate. There's always a price to pay, isn't there? But the 'Cointreau' consoled me, and moreover needed no instructions. There's no better nightcap, round the dying embers, with a few roasted chestnuts.

City Limits

Greed took us to Montpellier, a creamy-white and flourishing city almost on the Mediterranean shore. Word had gone round one January that a certain grocer in the city had Seville oranges in stock. Hot news!

It's not always easy to drag ourselves over the hills and far away, to slough off the narrowing mentality that living in a valley clothes us in. It needs carrot or stick, spur or sweetener, to get us off our haunches and into the car. It's difficult, too, to conceive that it might just be possible for any expat Brit to do without marmalade at breakfast, and marmalade, of course, is a complete non-runner in the French breakfast stakes. Few drool over breakfast here. Scents of frying bacon never sharpen the sweet Languedoc morning air. *Le petit déjeuner* stays hidden behind closed shutters, a furtive, unseen thing. I once made a mini-survey of the breakfast habits of several people I knew, with the following results:

Joseph Brolly, retired smallholder: *Un bol* (a bowl large enough to take three good cupfuls) of hot chocolate, into which he dunked the previous day's bread, slightly stale but not rock-hard.

Lionel Poussines, former bank clerk: *Un bol* of chocolate, like Joseph, but he dunked *un toast* into it. (*Un toast* is pre-toasted bread, something like a baby's rusk but more brittle.)

Jean-Michel Roumegous, architect: A *café militaire* and the other half of the cigar he'd started in bed the night before.

Eric Benoist, insurance broker: M. Benoist was a special case. A committed Anglophile, he believed he was breakfasting *à l'anglaise* in taking unmilked tea, into which he dunked his toast spread with orange jam, followed by a fried egg.

César Desjoyeaux, estate agent: We've already heard about César's daily *pain au chocolat*, which he dunked in *un bol* of coffee, although we once tried to persuade him that porridge might be effective in reducing his cholesterol level. We gave him some oatmeal with instructions, but from his evasive and non-committal answers when we asked him about it we deduced that this introduction to oat cuisine hadn't been a success. Old breakfast habits, like old jokes, die hard.

Indeed they do. Apart from M. Benoist's Anglo-Saxon flirtation with orange jam, not at all the same thing as marmalade, none of these Frenchmen had the slightest involvement with Seville oranges. So difficult were they to find that at one time we seriously considered driving to Seville for them. But that was before we heard about M. Pinto, the Montpellier grocer.

Montpellier? It's not an enormous town, but it passes for the ninth or tenth most populous place in a land not noted for huge cities. It's a 90-minute drive from Olargues, and there's always that subconscious heart-searching as we climb away from the security of the valley, up and over the last hills before the sea, cross the unending patchwork of vineyards, skeletal and whiskery in the winter sun, with maybe a glimpse of the distant Pyrenees, before we reach the A9, the *autoroute* that they call La Languedocienne. It follows the northern shore of the Mediterranean, one of history's great highways and now one of its great commercial arteries. Immediately we're plunged into a new world, a world of feverish top-speed economic activity, the European

Union for real, in constant transit: trailered juggernauts hammering out the kilometres from Lisbon to Milan, Toulouse to Vienna, Barcelona to Hamburg . . . and, we hoped, Seville to Montpellier.

The approach to Montpellier from the south-east takes us through one of the most exciting city developments we know. It's not an old city, as Rome or London are old. It only became an administrative centre of the Languedoc after the decline of Pézenas in the late 17th-century, although there'd been an important medical school there since the 1300s. The city really took off with the return from North Africa of so many French colonials in the 1960s. Someone with broad vision, a broader drawing-board and a yet broader purse conceived a city to house them and their aspirations. The Catalan architect Ricardo Bofill was engaged, and filled a quarter called Antigone with city vistas on a grand scale, with elegant buildings in the neo-Classical style using a creamy-white biscuity composite stone/concrete that perfectly complements the Midi luminescence. Fountains, avenues, gardens . . . we wonder if there's a pleasanter city anywhere round the Mediterranean.

The traffic flows reasonably freely, too. If you're bound for the city centre, suddenly an underpass leads you to a multi-level underground car-park. When you surface, you find yourself, again, in a different world: you're in the Place de la Comédie, surely one of the most beautiful, most sophisticated city centres in Europe.

What strikes first is the silence. There's no traffic; it's all taken underground. What noise there is comes from footsteps on the marble paving, from the tinkle of coffee cups and *pastis* glasses on the café *terrasses*, which spread far wider on to the square than traffic would allow. This is where shirt-sleeved *Montpelliérains* sit out in the January sun, listening to buskers who never seem intrusive in a square the size of several football pitches: Afro-French drum and saxophone duos, earnest music students playing Mozart, a flamenco guitarist working the café tables, and the bigger the donation the more flashing the smile. An old-fashioned roundabout, with painted horses that ride up and down, adds a few quavers of fairground music to the symphony of a city centre wonderfully free of the traffic banished to the Hades beneath. How sane, how civilised.

The name, the Place de la Comédie, is explained at the western end, the focal point of the square. Here stands the Opéra-Comédie, the municipal opera-house and theatre, a majestic Second Empire palace, so wedding-cake ornate that you feel you could break bits off and nibble them. If you look out over the square from the Opéra balcony you can easily feel positively imperial, as if the throng below owed you homage. There's an unreality about it, as though the scene below you was an opera being performed in the square instead of on the stage inside. In winter, after sunset, the square is brilliantly lit by a white light with a touch of frost to it. With the silver and gold Christmas decorations, which last from November to mid-February here, it's like being part of an immense, living Christmas card.

But we came for Seville oranges. Much of the city centre is pedestrianised, and it's a short traffic-free and fumeless walk from the Place de la Comédie up the Rue de la Loge, passing a sports shoe shop called The Athlete's Foot (d'you think they *know?* we ask ourselves, giggling), and into the Rue de l'Argenterie, where M. Pinto's shop is heralded by mingled scents of spices, cinnamon, turmeric, cardamom, saffron, cloves. And there, spilling out on to the pavement with boxes of other exotica – mangoes, pecans, couscous, pomegranates – were the rumoured Seville oranges.

'*Attention! C'est spécial, ça!*' an assistant inside warned us, explaining that these oranges were fit only for making jam. '*Spécial*' can carry derogatory overtones, 'peculiar' or even 'weird'. We came clean: making jam was exactly what we wanted them for. Our accents gave us away, and M. Pinto – for it was he – divined the Great British Breakfast Need and hastened out, all nods and becks and wreathèd smiles, to weigh out the 15kg that would keep us going until the next January. A glance round his shop revealed his familiarity with British tastes, because his shelves groaned with goodies not usually available in France – custard powder, pickles, fruit cake, baked beans, creamed rice pudding, mint sauce, Christmas puddings – all at a price. You don't corner the market in expat supplies and give the stuff away.

We returned to the Place de la Comédie at the time the French call *entre chien et loup*, between dog and wolf, just at dusk, when there were hints of another, darker side to Montpellier. As we passed McDonalds we were surprised to see black-uniformed security guards, and as the evening crept on the generally well-heeled crowds dispersed and the *marginaux* (down-and-outs) took their place, their indispensable dogs taking on a more wolfish air. The fountains, topped with classical statuary, began to fill with lager cans and *mégots*, fag-ends. Street corner gangs formed. There was probably little harm in them, but we were aware of a police presence we hadn't noticed before. Suddenly the other France showed itself, the France of the urban have-nots, the France where *liberté*, *égalité* and *fraternité* don't rub shoulders.

Time to go home. There was a lot be said for Olargues, after all. And for marmalade for breakfast.

MUSIC

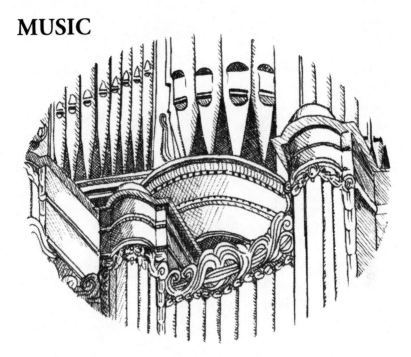

All Together Now – Un Deux Trois

They were already singing when the choir bus stopped to pick us up a little way along the road to Albi. As usual, the younger sopranos had annexed the back seat, and the other 45-odd choir members were distributed up and down the bus: René, leading tenor and chief of the local forest fire service; Jean, the retired stonemason, who's never worn socks in his life and clearly isn't going to start today, Festival or no Festival; Michel, wine merchant and seedsman; Bernard, shelf-stacker and trolley-recoverer from Marché U, the local supermarket; and so on up to the front seat, shared by plump and ever-laughing Mimi and beautiful Josie, head of the private

Catholic school in St Pons de Thomières, usually shortened to St Pons.

Everyone invited us to sit near them, patting vacant seats encouragingly. I sat for a while next to Mizou, short for Marie-Elise, who runs the local youth theatre group. She told me that her teenage son had just returned from 'Pairss'. Pairss? She meant Perth, in Scotland, where he'd been with a St Pons school group. Was my former home near there? I told her it was about 200 kilometres further north. '*Oh là-là*,' she said, 'it must be the North Pole . . .'

So the Chorale du Pays de Thomières, to give the choir its Sunday name, rolled on singing through the exquisite Midi countryside, drowsily lush and warm in the spring sun, towards Albi, a beautiful pepper-pink town on the banks of the river Tarn, a chief place of the Languedoc and guardian of its rich heritage. Here was the venue of an annual Festival called *Per Joia Recomençar* (Let's do it again for the pleasure) and switched-on language buffs will recognise instantly that this isn't French. No, it's Occitan or *patois*, as the local people call it, the ancient language of the Languedoc (in fact, purists prefer to call it *languedocien*), not too far removed from the Latin which the Romans brought here 2000 years ago. It's widely – and proudly – spoken, especially by the older people, and of course sung too, for the vein of Occitan folk-song is very rich indeed, amply rich enough to sustain an annual choir festival dedicated to it.

We arrive, one of 14 invited choirs from all over the Languedoc. A quick rehearsal on the stage, then outside into the evening for the main pre-concert business: a buffet meal provided by the organisers, with help-yourself wine from the barrel. There's much laughter and wishing of *bon appetit*.

The Festival finally starts at 9 pm. With 14 choirs, each with their allotted 10 minutes, plus an interval and grand finale, it's likely to be a long night. There's a manic compère, linking each choir by interviewing its conductor, thrusting his microphone at his victims like a rapier. In Occitan. I understand about one word in twenty. All I can say with confidence is *va plan?* pronounced 'ba plà'. *Va plan* is much the same as the French *ça va*, which you can make mean all kinds of things according to your inflexion: *how are you?* . . . *how are things?* . . . *OK* . . . *fine* . . . *fair to middling* . . . *that's quite enough, thank you*, and so on. I'm going to have to run the full gamut of inflexions if he insists on interviewing me.

Our choir is on last, the programme tells us, so there's a long nervous wait through the thirteen other choirs. Some are good, some mediocre, and I know our choir won't disgrace itself. Particularly enchanting is a group of children from the local school of traditional music who are singing and playing hurdy-gurdies.

At ten past midnight our turn comes, and I lead the St Pons choir up to the stage, feeling a desperate fraud because the moment I open my mouth, even to say *va plan?*, my accent will betray me as a sneaking interloper, not even French. What I'm doing here conducting this choir and teaching them their own songs is another story, hard enough to explain in French, let alone Occitan. The manic compère edges closer, fixing me with his glittering eye, his microphone twitching like a dowser's rod. Michel, practised Occitan speaker, senses the emergency and deftly interposes himself between me and the microphone. I'm saved. *Va plan.*

I lift my baton and we launch into *Diguo, Janeto* (Tell me, Janet) which they sing perfectly from memory. A plus for St Pons, although it's not a competitive festival: all the other choirs except the children have had sheet music. Then *La Lauzeto* (The Lark). They're in good form. I needn't have worried. Then *O up! As pas entendut?* (Hey, haven't you heard?). Crisp, accurate singing. The choir's enjoying it. Just as well: if they don't enjoy it, how can they expect anyone else to? All that work in rehearsal every Tuesday night has been worth it. Finally, the lively, toe-tapping Farandole:

> *On s'enchau d'anar descauç*
> *Mai que l'on manje, mai que l'on bouje*

(Who cares if we go barefoot, as long as there's plenty to eat and drink?)

The audience begins to clap in time to the music. I make the choir sing it again, and the audience, by degrees, starts waving arms, dancing, stamping, conga-ing between the seats. I remember the golden rule: always leave your audience wanting more. I bring the choir to a halt. Wild applause. *Bravo*, St Pons: you've done yourselves – and me – proud. An unknown woman rushes out of the audience to kiss me on both cheeks. It was never like this in Scotland.

They sang all the way back, led again from the rear by the sopranos. They included, especially for us, the only song they knew by heart in English: *Away in a manger.*

Wonderful. I hope we're invited back again next year. *Per Joia Recomençar*, you know.

Gabriel Fauré's Organ

Roger Calmel was the composer who arranged, among many other songs for choirs to sing, *Diguo, Janeto* and *O up! As pas entendut?* which we sang at the Albi festival. He's no longer with us, at least not in the flesh: he died in Paris in 1998 after a distinguished musical career, teaching, broadcasting, performing, but especially composing music that time is assessing to see how well he stands comparison with the immortals of French music. Nowhere is he more lamented and more missed than in Creissan, his native village, on the Languedoc plain not far from Béziers.

But if he made it by the fast track then he's probably over there beyond the last horizon somewhere, strolling through the Elysian Fields talking with Debussy and Berlioz, looking forward to the *apéritif* later on with Ravel and Offenbach – and maybe a night out with the lads, César, Georges and Gabriel. César Franck, Georges Bizet and Gabriel Fauré, that is, the same Gabriel Fauré whose *Requiem* has probably ensured him a place in the Panthéon of French composers on all counts.

Heaven knows what they might be talking about. Cooking, as likely as not, one of Roger's other strings to his bow. He'll be doing the talking: he wasn't much of a listener. In fact he often seemed reluctant to respond to outside stimuli. For years he called me Cristobal. Reminding him became such a chore that I gave up, reckoning it was easier for us both if I chucked in the baptismal sponge. If ever I rang him up I would say *Bonjour, Roger, c'est Cristobal* and there would be a cry of instant recognition the other end. Once when I was in Cape Town I sent him a postcard of Table Mountain, one of the world's more instantly recognisable views. A few weeks later he thanked me most courteously for a souvenir of Labastide. I expect his head was so full of music trying to get out that anything trying to get in risked being trampled to death in the crush.

He came into my little world of village choirs in a roundabout way. Some years ago a local Senator, Raoul Bayou, had the idea of creating a music festival to link the vineyard, olive grove and cherry orchard communities along the banks of the river Orb and its tributaries. Le Festival de la Vallée de l'Orb was born, a month-long series of summer concerts in local churches, wine cellars, community centres and out-of-doors in village parks. Local choirs were approached to prepare a choral work, which the massed choirs would perform under the baton of a big name in French music. Who better than Roger Calmel, a local lad?

Roger agreed, and for several years made a monthly journey from Paris to Creissan to rehearse the massed *choristes* from places with magical, sun-caressed names – St Chinian, Magalas-Pouzolles, Thézan-lès-Béziers, Sérignan, St Pons de Thomières – whose choirmasters were conscripted into the tenors and basses when he took the rostrum, and I became his rehearsal pianist and concert accompanist.

He wasn't always easy to work with. He unerringly chose big-match – rugby or football – Saturday afternoons to rehearse on, and then complained bitterly of the absence of men. He was fidgety, imperious and quite capable of losing his place and then blaming the altos for breathing at the wrong point when everything ground to a halt. There would be mutinous mutterings when, frustrated with slow progress, he held up his Parisian choirs as examples of disciplined, quick-learning excellence.

The performance to be dreaded was the annual offering to Le Festival de la Vallée de l'Orb in Creissan, his own village, which he insisted on giving out of doors in a small park with a covered stage next to the municipal camping site. A few summer evening sounds complemented his music: crickets singing into the night, distant church bells, wheeling swallows twittering in the upper air. Most didn't: Roger would perform blithely through thunderstorms, gales, the local youth revving its motorbikes, Dutch campers improvising basketball games, a fishmonger's mobile shop loudspeaker announcing the day's bargains.

One evening, when the north wind, the *tramontane*, tore indiscriminately at sheet music, concert hair-dos and unweighted skirt-hems, Roger found himself unable to keep his scores on the conductor's desk, a further aggravation to one who often lost his place. A tall figure not without authority, he beckoned a surprised child from the audience, whom he made to stand in front of him for the rest of the evening, holding up the music tightly. On another occasion, an elderly lady fell backwards over a low parapet into an ornamental well in the middle of the auditorium. Gasps of horror from the audience, a rush by those nearest to pull her out. Luckily, a grille prevented her from falling very far, and although very shaken she wasn't really hurt. Lost in the music Roger carried on, completely oblivious to the commotion behind him.

Perhaps because of this total absorption in and commitment to his music, people loved him; they grumbled frightfully but turned up year after year to sing for him.

The major work for each year was chosen the previous August, a month he spent alone in his family house in Creissan, far from his Paris *conservatoire* work and a busy international conducting schedule. I was surprised to be summoned to lunch one day: Roger announced that he was going to cook duck *à l'orange* for his lieutenants, his choir conductors, Louis Ducourant of St Chinian, Robert Ganidel of Magalas, Jo Garcia of Thézan-lès-Béziers, Michel Verdier of Sérignan, François Nougaret of Bédarieux and me, and afterwards we could discuss next year's programme. A great honour.

The *apéritif* was served in his work-room, which was sparsely furnished, a big table, an elderly piano and in one corner an old harmonium. Roger showed me the composition he was working on: he'd been commissioned to write a musical celebration for Tours cathedral of the 1500th anniversary of the city's patron, St Martin. He'd taken the notes of a peal of the cathedral bells as the basis for part of his cantata. He pointed out the notes of the peal in his tiny manuscript, and told me how he'd adapted them for singing voices and instruments, a fascinating insight into the working habits of a first division composer. He moved over to the piano to let me hear what he'd been working on. The piano was horribly out of tune, a real honky-tonk job, and I wondered how it was possible that the delicacy of his musical hearing wasn't constantly offended by this jangling cacophony. Oh, he'd got used to it, he said, his ear corrected it and he didn't notice it any more. Pianos in the Midi were like that: the wooden frames once favoured by French piano manufacturers couldn't stand the dry climate, they couldn't take the tension of the strings. Better this old family piano than that *thing* over there, he said, using *machin* for 'thing', pointing to the dusty harmonium. In the past he used to clear the *loirs* out of it when he arrived each August, but now he didn't bother any more. They'd gnawed too many of its vitals and it didn't work, bar a few notes.

A family instrument too? I asked. No, Roger replied carelessly, as though we'd been talking about a pair of old shoes he was going to throw out, it had belonged to Gabriel Fauré. Fauré had used it to compose *Le Cantique de Jean Racine* on. Did I know it? A flawless composition, a work of the greatest beauty . . . but suddenly the duck *à l'orange* needed his attention and he disappeared into the kitchen. At lunch, which was excellent, the talk was of other things and I never found out how Gabriel Fauré's organ came into Roger's possession.

Roger died of cancer in Paris ten months later, on the day the festival concert was due to be given in Creissan, and it fell to François and me to take the massed choirs through the programme he'd put together. For once, nothing went wrong, though the concert seemed empty and pointless without him. The choirs sang at his funeral in Creissan a few days later, and we shared dinner that evening with some of his Paris *choristes*, who were delighted to meet at last some members of the Languedoc choir he used to hold up to them as such an example of discipline and quickness to learn . . .

We put on a memorial concert for him the following year, and once again the little park at Creissan was filled with his music on a perfect evening, warm and still. At one stage a cat strolled across the auditorium in front of the audience, stopped suddenly, as cats do, to lick its hind parts energetically, and stalked on. At a poignant, hushed moment in Roger's cantata *Le Sous-Préfet aux Champs* a hen in somebody's backyard announced to all Creissan the arrival of that day's egg. The choirs sang on, undeterred.

Roger's spirit was with us yet.

The Late Late Show

At nine o'clock, just when the concert is due to begin, we're still sitting round Frédérique's table, with the débris of supper, among them a *colin*, a whole hake, baked tail-in-mouth, scattered about us.

We Brits, still uneasy about shaking off the tyranny of the clock despite living in the unpunctual Midi for several years, begin to fidget. Oughtn't we to be moving? Aren't we going to be terribly late? Frédérique, president of the concert-sponsoring Friends of the Olargues Organ, is in no hurry. She seems determined to be late. We fret in vain. You can't very well speed the parting host, especially when you're pleasantly full of her *colin*.

And late we are. In Scotland we would have turned tail and gone home, unable to face the shame of it. Even what they call *le petit quart d'heure méditerranéen,* the little Mediterranean quarter of an hour, which usually elapses between the advertised start of an event and its actual getting under way, hasn't saved us. We are very late indeed. As we approach the church in Olargues, on foot because the old village streets are too narrow to take cars, we can hear that the concert has already begun: there's someone singing, a rich and creamy soprano, but distant and muffled through the ancient masonry. We tiptoe in, and of course the door creaks abominably, drawing unwelcome attention. The church is full. There are no seats left. We're the last. We're obliged to perch on a marble balustrade at the back, just inside the door.

She's billed as Theodora Ciucur, *prima donna* with the Timisoara Opera. I wonder what possible chain of circumstances can have wafted her from provincial Romania to humble Olargues, but there she is, just above us in the little gallery next to the organ: no sylph, but a deep-bosomed lady of Wagnerian full habit. She can sing, no question.

As we creep in she's in full flow from Messiah: *He shall feed his flock.* Mme Ciucur has a little difficulty with her English: *E shell gezzer ze lembs weez eez arm* (which can't be so very different from Handel's own pronunciation, surely?) and it's strangely moving to hear something so nostalgically British, composed by a German, sung in France by a Romanian. But any starting tear of homesickness is quickly dispelled by a bizarre circumstance.

Mme Ciucur has sensibly chosen to sing from a position next to the organ, in order to be as close to her accompanist as possible. In Olargues church the organ gallery is mounted high on the back wall of the church. As you might expect, all the pews face forward, towards the brilliantly lit altar. The entire audience, wedged together tightly in the pews, has to sit with its back to her. Except ourselves, on our marble perch. We're the only ones who can see her.

As the concert continues she gets fully into her operatic stride, pouring out the vintage *bel canto* like the fine Bordeaux we helped down Frédérique's supper with. Olargues can have heard nothing like this before: clearly the folk of Timisoara like their opera hot and strong. With each burst of enthusiastic applause, directed necessarily towards the plaster saints round the altar, she can only respond to that part of the audience actually facing her, i.e. ourselves, with bobs and bows and smiles and occasionally a blown kiss for Marcel, Frédérique's father, whom we've met before as the elderly interpreter in the M. Gonzales – Mademoiselle Irina affair. He's having a wonderful time. He seems very taken with the lady. Frédérique elbows him crossly from time to time, but it makes no difference: he might be an aged Romeo playing the balcony scene.

As usual after village concerts, there's a reception in the Mairie. By rights we deserve only the final crumbs, but Frédérique too gezzers her lembs hastily and shepherds us hotfoot down the narrow street, making an astounding assertion on the way: as President of the Friends of the Organ she must be first to welcome the guests. I search for the French to frame the obvious question with the maximum courtesy: *Mais comment se passe-t-il . . . ?* But how does it happen that . . . ?

'I know what you're going to say,' she cuts in. 'Wasn't it wonderful, being able to see her? No one else could, you know. Well worth being late for, don't you think?'

Most of the audience reassembles at the Mairie, plastic beaker in hand, queuing at the self-service barrels of local *rouge* or *rosé,* or helping themselves from the bottles of the excellent muscat these Languedoc hills produce. Mme Ciucur is there, beaming benignly at everyone from her place of honour next to M. Arcas the *maire*. Marcel has lost no time in attending to her needs with an old-world grace, continuing a courtly flirtation started in the church in what seems to be Latin.

One o'clock strikes, some of the guests have gone, the organist's children have fallen asleep on the floor, and Frédérique sharply tells her father to knock off the *amo amas amat* because what Mme Ciucur really needs is to get off to her bed, alone. Crestfallen, Marcel lingers over *la bise*, and we make our farewells and disappear into the night. The crickets are still singing.

A few days later we're on concert duty again in Béziers cathedral for a farewell recital given by Victoria de los Angeles, a truly *grande dame* of – well, much the same age as Marcel, who is quivering with an excitement we aren't sure is purely musical. The cathedral is packed, but the occasion is more nostalgic than uplifting: there are no more than embers from those magical *Songs of the Auvergne*, no more than a few final sparks from the world's finest Carmen of the 50s and 60s. At least we're all facing her.

At the end Marcel says to me, conspiratorially, out of Frédérique's hearing, '*Ah, si seulement . . .*' If only. . . I nod and smile. There's no need to say more.

Night Of The Lithuanians

There was an unscheduled interruption to the weekly rehearsal of the Olargues choir when Achmed walked in: gradually the hum of low conversation endemic in a choir largely made up of teachers, social workers and beekeepers came to a halt. Achmed had something to say.

Achmed is the local *percepteur*, the tax collector, a man whose lot is to view mankind with constant suspicion, frustration and disappointment.

You wonder what he might have done in a previous existence to deserve posting to the tax desk in Olargues – until you remember that it's by his own will, presumably, that he opens the doors of the Trésor Public in the rue des Ecoles every morning and that he could just as well have been a teacher, social worker or indeed a beekeeper, if he'd put his mind to it.

Anyway the village choir came up to scratch in Achmed's purview of the human race, although his visit had nothing to do with taxes. He was looking for hosts for some visitors from Lithuania, in fact a 50-strong choir sensibly wanting to exchange its native Baltic fogs and frosts for the sun of the Midi for a few days. Who had a spare bed?

The choir shuffled awkwardly and began to excuse itself from offering B&B to a couple of Lithuanian tenors or a trio of sopranos. Admittedly the notice was very short, and maybe Achmed wasn't the best person to choose as a billeting officer. Wherever the Lithuanian choir laid its weary head, it wasn't Olargues.

However, they did come and sing for us in the village church, and some of the village choir agreed to provide a short programme as a curtain-raiser, including a rather *risqué* blues-ish men-only number roughly translatable as *Hell This Ain't My Bed I've Woke Up In And If This Is My Woman She Don't Smell Too Good,* not really the sort of thing to delight the plaster saints round the altar. But no Baltic susceptibilities were offended, it seemed, and Franco-Lithuanian relations continued intact, I expect because few of the visiting choir spoke French and anyway while this was going on they were preparing at the back of the church for their entry.

And what an entry! They processed down the aisle, tenors and basses first, smartly suited, tall, proud and assured, followed by a stately line of some 30 stunning blonde ice-maidens in national costume, long skirts, colourful pinafores, patterned shawls and flat tambour head-dresses embroidered with beads. Olargues gasped, especially the men of the choir when they saw what they'd missed in turning Achmed down.

Goodness, they could sing. Admittedly, it was harmless stuff about little birds and pine forests, spring sunshine and winter firesides, but they had a standing ovation and repeated calls for encores that were only stilled by the conductor marching his troops off.

But this was by no means the end of the evening. It never is, in the Midi. In fact, the official entertainment is often just a preliminary formality before settling down to the real business. The *maire* of Olargues, Jean Arcas, very kindly invited everyone to a reception in the Mairie. His actual words were *un verre de l'amitié*, a glass of friendship, which is always on the house, although there's usually a hidden charge in having to listen to the inevitable speeches.

M. Arcas called a sort of platform party round him, beneath the sightless gaze of Marianne and the official portrait of the President which hangs in every Mairie in France. Achmed was there, smiling uncertainly, among other village notables. The Lithuanian conductor, Jonas Vytautas Pavilonis, was called forward, together with the interpreter. M. Arcas warmed up, excitedly pointing out unexpected parallels between the Languedoc and Lithuania: 'We shook off the tyrant's yoke!' Perhaps he was referring to similarities between the French Revolution and the end of Soviet domination of the Baltic republics. How the interpreter, a rather shy Lithuanian teacher of French, translated this I don't know. Her spoken French wasn't confident, and M. Arcas' accent was very strong. All the same, the massed Balts nodded appreciatively. 'We defied the Nazi scourge!' M. Arcas went on. The Midi is immensely – and rightly – proud of the Resistance in World War 2. Was there a Lithuanian equivalent? If there was, the ice-maidens were much too young to remember it. Then: 'Our wines, second to none, must be tasted!'

This seemed a wide claim, to say the least. Although Languedoc wines are often excellent, and although the grapes from villages in the Olargues *canton* are harvested under the thoroughly respectable *appellation* St Chinian, there's no denying that they don't command quite the same prices as the best Burgundies or clarets. However, M. Arcas' pronouncement earned an enthusiastic round of applause mingled with cheers from the justifiably thirsty tenors and basses. Later it appeared that the interpreter had translated M. Arcas' pronouncement as 'I declare the bar open', or words to that effect, but it was a popular move: a barrel of the region's second-to-none *rouge* had been sprung, a rank of *pastis* bottles awaited their inevitable destiny, the council table groaned with fresh crisp *baguettes* and slices of pizza from M. Gosset, the Olargues baker, and a selection of cheeses, sausage and pâtés to persuade the hungriest singing Balt that the Midi was just down the road from the Garden of Eden.

But it also appeared that the Lithuanians had brought their own refreshment, just in case. Who could blame them? All they knew about Olargues was that no one had been prepared to accommodate them, and who knew if they were going to be fed and watered? So manna from the Midi was matched with benison from the Baltic, so to speak, and the Olarguais began to mingle, not unwillingly, with the massed ice-maidens, still in their national costume, while their tenors and basses circulated with a quite unexpected commodity: Lithuanian wine, a light sparkling white that soon co-operated with the local *rouge* to work its magic, and from the resulting noise you wouldn't have guessed that neither Balt nor Latin had a common language. It didn't matter much, because one of the Lithuanians produced a chat-drowning accordion, and presently the council chamber trembled with polkas and waltzes so rapid that you weren't certain whether you were spinning round the room or the room was spinning round you or whether that was the seventh or the sixteenth ice-maiden who'd just whizzed past, pinafore flying.

At this point the Lithuanian whisky began to circulate too, at about the same time as M. Arcas decided it was high time he sang a little song, an exercise of mayoral privilege nobody would have minded if he hadn't summoned Claude Rudel, an amiable local *vigneron* and principal bass of the Olargues choir, and myself to help him sing the *Se Canto*, a chronically gloomy Occitan song about lost love that has somehow become an unofficial Midi anthem. Useless to hide among the ice-maidens: M. Arcas hadn't become first citizen of Olargues not to see things through to their conclusion. The applause was muted and brief.

More dancing, more singing, more toasting of Franco-Lithuanian friendship, more *bonhomie* until the belfry above the Mairie rang out midnight and Jonas Vytautas Pavilonis gathered his myrmidons and ice-maidens about him and shepherded them off. 'So soon, Maestro Pavilonis?' I asked him, having discovered that he spoke a little English. He pressed me to visit him in Lithuania at any time with any choir I might happen to have about me, but excused himself and his singers: it was the last night of their tour and *they had a party to go to.*

Just A Song At Twilight

'The theme of the evening,' said the woman who seemed to be in charge, 'is *l'Art du Feu*, the Art of Fire.'

To make the point clear she handed me an armful of *flambeaux*, torches of wax-impregnated wadding wrapped round a stick. About a dozen, not nearly enough to supply all the choir members. Just as well, maybe: you can't hold a flaming torch in one hand and your music folder in the other. But then, how were they going to see in the dark? I expected we would improvise, get by somehow or other. We were well used to it.

A day or two before I'd had a call from the Mairie asking if the choir I conduct, Le Choeur des Hauts Cantons, could possibly perform in one of the evening events they drum up at short notice in Olargues for their annual August *fête* days. Could we manage a few songs in each of several locations around the village, alternating with declamations from local poets?

I said I'd ask. Le Choeur des Hauts Cantons was a new choir, just about to celebrate its first birthday. Choirs form and reform here, amoeba-like in their reproduction. My association with Le Choeur du Pays de Thomières ended when I came to live in Olargues. Marcelle, the plump and pleasing alto whose grandson was last seen at work in the St Pons dump, signed up with the new choir and suggested that we call ourselves The Choir of the High Cantons, the name sometimes given to this area of hill settlements.

A quick scramble in the branches of our *arbre téléphonique*, the telephone tree, the system of who calls whom for short-order business, and it was arranged: the choir would meet at the foot of the Commanderie steps at 9 pm.

Olargues lends itself to happenings like *l'Art du Feu*. The old village descends defensively by steep tier and terrace from the *château*, of which only the bell tower remains, on the rocky hilltop overhanging the river. The old quarter is rich in narrow alleys, arches, tiny flowered courts, vaulted tunnels and old stone-built houses built into the parent rock, where the back door takes you into the attic and the front door opens on to the cobbled lane two or three floors below. There's no traffic: everywhere's much too narrow. The old quarter is rich in flights of steps, too: one of the principal village thoroughfares is the Escalier de la Commanderie, a covered stone stairway leading up six flights from the rue Neuve to the rue Mégeane and the church door. At its foot, shortly before 9 pm, I dumped my *flambeaux* and other accoutrements, sheet music, music stand, tuning fork, maracas and tambourine, and waited for the choir to assemble, wondering what we were going to sing.

This posed a problem: nothing in our repertoire, really quite limited after a mere year in existence, was remotely connected with *l'Art du Feu*. Dragonflies on the Moon, Thwarted Love, The Bosom of Abraham – nothing's too far-fetched to have songs written about it – we could do these at the drop of a hat. But the Art of Fire? Well, too bad. In any case the Art of Fire seemed to be as much about getting the *flambeaux* to burn as anything else: it needed a steady application from our accompanist Gilbert (pronounced Zheel-bair) the guitarist's lighter to get them going. Once lit they gave out a pleasant, flickering light that looked very pretty from a distance, even if they stank of paraffin wax close to and blackened your hands as you held them. However, many choir members had brought friends and relations with them, who were quickly press-ganged into bearing torches for us, thus thrusting the flame of culture into dark places, as you might say. Problem solved: this would be the Art of Fire. What we sang was immaterial.

The poets arrived, fifteen or so of all ages and both sexes, a Live Poets' Society tricked out in white tops and black skirts or trousers with red accessories, their manuscripts peeping out of reticules, ample corsages or trouser pockets, pinned to the backs of fans or folded inside old leather-bound books. A pre-arranged plan clearly unfolded as they deployed themselves at a window here, in a doorway there, on somebody's front-door steps, amid the geraniums on somebody else's balcony. A sizeable crowd gathered in front of the Mairie, people from Olargues and the surrounding villages together with dozens of tourists, *flambeaux* aloft, all ready to be led in torchlight procession along the narrow streets and alleys from poet to poet.

We didn't hear them all, because the choir, due to sing in only four places, leapfrogged several poetry-points, from the *pontil*, a wooden bridge carrying the rue Mégeane over the lane below, back to the vaulted Commanderie stairway and its wonderfully resonant acoustics, along the rue Neuve to the Place du Vicomte, where we sang in Italian the only item in our repertoire with any possible relevance to the evening's theme: a little Mozart nocturne called *Luci care* (dear lights) and then – musical tastes are gratifyingly wide here – a fast Charleston number called *Madeleine*.

Night had fallen when we reached our final port of call, the Place des Trois Fontaines, chosen because it was close to a point where you could see, across the riverside gardens and rooftops, the hump-backed, centuries-old Pont du Diable, the Devil's Bridge. By the time we'd launched ourselves into our last item, a cracking arrangement of *Alexander's Ragtime Band*, translated into French as *L'Orchestre de Zazou*, the crowd had swelled to about 200. Little cameos remain: a boy of four or five shyly creeping up beside me and waving his arms about, imitating me conducting; a blonde woman in a pink bath towel at an upper window, nodding rhythmically; and the most *sympathique*, Père Merle, the almost-blind *curé* of Olargues, jigging, twitching and clapping like everyone else in time to the music.

As the last notes died away, fireworks erupted from the floodlit Pont du Diable, rockets and Roman candles in fountains of fire, bringing the Art of Fire to a splendid climax.

Happy days, happy nights. Maybe the poets will write about it one day.

EVENTS

Follow That Caveman

Scattered about St Pons are little signs with *troglodytes* (cavemen) on them, stomping along purposefully. If you too stomp along purposefully, obeying the *suivez-moi* (follow me) instruction under each one, you'll end up in the Musée Préhistoire, and waiting on the steps to greet you may be the aptly-named – on account of his beatific presence and angelic smile – Gabriel Rodriguez.

M. Rodriguez is impassioned by the megaliths, the dolmens and menhirs with which the St Pons area abounds, evidence of a stone-age Mediterranean culture which archaeologists recognise as St Ponien. These relics, of which more and more are coming to light throughout the Western Mediterranean area, are the subject of a growing school of archaeological study and research, to which one of M. Rodriguez' contributions was the organisation of *Le Deuxième Colloque International sur le Statuaire Mégalithique*, the 2nd International Symposium on Megalithic Statuary. Heady stuff for St Pons.

The opening ceremony of the *Deuxième Colloque* (an interesting word which M. Rodriguez pronounced almost like *clock*) was held in the auditorium of the Maison du Pays. I once went there to see the film *Germinal* as part of a public so unexpectedly numerous that extra seating had to be commandeered in the form of plastic chairs from neighbouring gardens. This time, too, the audience was substantial, but then to ensure a good gate M. Rodriguez had taken the sensible precaution of inviting the St Pons choir and their partners, baiting the hook with promise of a *buffet campagnard* afterwards, which I suppose you could translate as country sideboard. No event of this kind in France is complete without a meal.

There were suspiciously more people at the *buffet campagnard* than had sat through a long hour's-worth of speeches in the Maison du Pays, although the pace quickened towards the end when M. Rodriguez suggested it was easier squeezing blood out of a megalith than getting money for his *Deuxième Colloque* out of the St Pons *maire*, or words to that effect. Violent reaction from Kléber Mesquida, the able and hard-working *maire* of St Pons, hotly resenting any slur on his town's dedication to megalithic studies in front of delegates from all over Europe, not to mention the St Pons Rent-a-Choir. Any breach was soon healed, however, in the ambience of *bonhomie*, *camaraderie* and *joie de vivre* at the country sideboard on the Terrasse du Jaur, a wooded terrace overlooking the cavern from which the river Jaur, already adult, flows out of the hillside. The air was sweet, the evening velvet, the music provided by the St Pons *groupe folklorique* elemental enough for any caveman to stomp purposefully to. As for the *buffet campagnard*, you could help yourself to as much as you wanted from the vast abundance of the cooked and cured meats in which the region is so rich, wonderfully varied salads, local cheeses and *pâtisseries* – and keep coming back for more. One of the magical things about these public meals is that as soon as a bottle is finished, it's instantly replaced.

To our shame we were among the last to leave, a contented, enthusiastically pro-megalith party consisting of friends from

Scotland, wide-eyed at this public plenty, Kléber Mesquida, Cathy the St Pons window cleaner, Mme Granier the self-appointed Franco-British liaison officer and Ian Kinnes, sole British Museum delegate, a Dundonian who was due to address the *colloque* the next morning. He showed us a demanding days' programme, opening with his paper on gender differences between menhirs, followed by a bus trip to Brassac, a tour on foot of the local megaliths, welcome by the *maire*, *buffet campagnard* at midday: in the afternoon, bus to Lacaune, tour of the local megaliths, *buffet campagnard* in the evening. Hard work, megalithic studies.

There's no such thing as a free meal, of course, and two evenings later the Rent-a-Choir did what it could to prevent the *Deuxième Colloque* from declining into a mere stagger from one *buffet campagnard* to another: we put on a concert in the cathedral. It falls to few to tailor a choral programme for an International Symposium on Megalithic Statuary, and I can't say I found it easy. However, our repertoire included one appropriate song, a negro spiritual called *Daniel Saw The Stone*. It went down very well. The delegates even applauded the title.

I don't know if the *Troisième Colloque* will be held in St Pons or elsewhere. Clearly *buffets campagnards* are a must for this sort of thing, but if in addition a choir's needed, one that knows what makes *colloques* tick, I'm sure they'd be happy to oblige.

The Chestnut Fair

Twenty-one thousand visitors is the highest figure to date. Spread over three days, of course, but still a huge number of incomers for a sleepy little place like St Pons.

It happens annually, on the last weekend in October: La Fête de la

Châtaigne, the Chestnut Fair. It's a street market, autumn fair, folk festival and harvest thanksgiving all rolled into one: local produce and craft stalls, invited folk-groups singing and dancing, sit-down meals in the marquee with cabaret entertainment, *loto* (bingo) to win a duck, a pig or a day trip to Andorra. A travelling fair with roundabouts and dodgems lustily wheezes out hearer-friendly 60s and 70s hits, *Ob-la-di* and *Chirpy-chirpy-cheep-cheep*. Roast chestnuts sell at a few *sous* the bag and the charred husks crunch underfoot. An *animateur*, a compère-cum-commentator, keeps everything bubbling away busily over speakers strategically placed round the town. There's noise, bustle, colour and fun. And the devil's own job to park.

Children come first on the Friday, a school day, but with a difference: departmental sports staff are drafted in to organise sports in the streets and open spaces, archery, mini-football, stilt-walking, basketball, wrestling. When children have had their turn of this they can move on to face-painting and dressing–up, and when all the robots, witches, clowns, dinosaurs or whatever's in fashion, from Teenage Mutant Hero Turtles to Teletubbies, are ready they parade up the street, round the cathedral, past the Mairie and back again, led by teachers who dress up too.

On Saturday and Sunday they light brushwood fires early, to provide a thick bed of glowing embers for chestnut roasting. Local worthies take turns to rotate big mesh drums, like giant spits, over the embers, stopping regularly to distribute enough chestnuts to keep the queue moving forward happily. Sometimes they're served in funnel-shaped pokes of paper torn from wallpaper sample books. There's a delicious scent in the air and *oh-là-làs!* as tingling fingers pick gingerly at the piping hot nuts.

France's best chestnuts are supposed to come from the St Ponais, the area round St Pons, and the pick go to make crystallised and sugared *marrons glacés*, a Christmas luxury here as elsewhere. Otherwise they're eaten as an autumn or winter speciality, either roasted or maybe braised in chicken stock, a delicious and unusual dish. In the past they were an indispensable winter staple, gathered by the sackful, smoke-dried and rid of any invading grubs in kilns called *sécadous* and milled into a flour which made a nourishing polenta, like a very smooth porridge. Specialist bakers, several of whom have their stalls at The Chestnut Festival, bake chestnut flour bread all year, and some local restaurants occasionally serve bread made of it. It has an individual taste, and a dryish texture somewhere between regular wheat wholemeal and rye bread.

Most of the lore surrounding chestnuts has passed into museums, possibly unregretted given the cussed nature of a crop you can barely touch without injuring yourself, although odd snippets may surface in referring to someone's stinginess: *Fork out for a round, him? Not likely – he's got chestnuts in his pocket!* Certainly the times when the local population depended on the annual chestnut crop aren't much more than a folk-memory now, like the costumes the people of St Pons trot out for La Fête de la Châtaigne: mob cap, shawl and much-petticoated long skirts for women, wide-brimmed black hat, red neckerchief, blue poncho and homespun or corduroy trousers for men, both with heavily nailed wooden *sabots* or clogs. Indeed one of the best-known local folk-songs, another of the many Occitan songs Roger Calmel arranged for choirs, is *Los Esclops*, The Clogs. It's a measure of the extreme localisation of the area that in St Pons the word is pronounced, as written, 'es-clops', while a few kilometres west, in Labastide in the next valley, they say 'es-clotch'. No prisoners are taken in this dialectal struggle: Bastidiens and St Ponais are always ready to defend their corners.

A linguist's delight, or nightmare? You could ask the same of the title of the flourishing St Pons folk-group, *Los Castagnaïres del Soumal*, The Chestnut Folk of the Somail (the range of hills north of St Pons) who perform songs, instrumental music and dances over the weekend together with other groups, even more exotically dressed, invited from neighbouring regions and from outside France. When *Los Castagnaïres* dance, with hobnails on metal stage, the noise is colossal, shattering. It would be more peaceful up in the cathedral belfry, on the hour.

There's no dancing, however, in the packed cathedral for the Festival Mass on the Sunday morning, but you can hardly miss the clog-clatter on the nave flagstones as the groups process in. Their accompanying music is splendidly barbaric to northern ears: the piercing reediness of shawms (a sort of primitive oboe), tattoos on neck-slung tabors, a giant single-droned bagpipe made out of a whole pigskin minus the head, so that the little legs stick out when the bag is inflated – this music, with more than a hint of Arabic North Africa, can't have changed for centuries.

Suddenly the clogs subside, giving way to a slow, dignified tap. The massive east doors of the cathedral have been flung wide to admit the most exotic group, floppy black hats, red neckerchiefs, white shirts and sheepskin jackets and . . . stilts. They're shepherds from the Landes, the area stretching south from Bordeaux towards the Basque country, a region so flat that stilts are necessary to double their height and increase their range of vision over their flocks. They process down the aisle carefully, deliberately, almost as though filmed in slow motion, each shepherd holding a long pole to lean on, to balance with and to help in mounting and dismounting, which they do very deftly, taking their bodyweight on their poles as they kneel to undo the straps of their stilts.

We see all this richness from the organ gallery, where La Chorale du Pays de Thomières is 'animating' the Mass. We can see, too, a procession of children in traditional costume coming up to the altar steps to offer baskets of local produce, apples, walnuts, brilliant orange persimmons, mushrooms, grapes, olives and, of course, the famous chestnuts. Yes, richness: suddenly Harvest Festivals don't seem so far away, after all. It's at this moment that we feel we abandon our roots in the soil, however vestigial, at our peril. Have we evolved anything much to replace them? I doubt it, and I suspect the 21,000 Chestnut Festival visitors might have their doubts too.

Rugby And Rhubarb

'*Cela est bien dit*,' says Candide in Voltaire's novel, '*mais il faut cultiver notre jardin.*' That's well said, but we must get on with our garden.

Yes, if only I could. There's nothing like a spadeful of literary compost to bring these pieces on, but as far as *notre jardin* is concerned I'm afraid there's sometimes severe neglect at the time of the annual Six Nations Rugby Championships. Just when gardens need most attention, too. If the distractions of rugby weren't enough, spring can be quite capricious here, with icy showers blown in by the *tramontane*, the snell blast from the north that sends drip-nosed locals scurrying for their shawls and *vestes*, i.e. grimy anoraks, as they wield the hoe and rake. If for once there's bright, warm sunshine, summoning me and my spade and fork from their winter quarters in the shed to trudge up the hill to *cultiver notre jardin*, France is bound to be meeting Scotland at rugby that afternoon and nothing will get done. Again.

Jardin isn't quite the right word, not for a vegetable garden. The French say *potager*, which literally means soup-er, where you grow what you put in your soup. In Olargues the *potagers* are some distance from the village, because the older houses are all built close-clustered, like hibernating snails, and there's no room for growing anything but the occasional wisteria, balcony tub of irises or window-box of geraniums. So the *potagers* are down by the river, which is a sensible arrangement because not only is the soil alluvial, fertile and easy to dig, but the water is plentiful and free. Too plentiful, sometimes: flood waters can wash away entire *potagers* and anything else in their path. I know of several trim riverside plots featuring ancient cars or vans firmly embedded in the alluvium. It's manna from heaven of a kind, I suppose, when flood waters deposit irremoveably a perfectly good Renault 4L van from somewhere upstream just where you were thinking of building a new potting shed. The valley of the river Salesse just south of St Pons is as much a museum of transport as a string of allotments. Nor is it only vehicles that are at risk: a couple of kilometres upstream from Olargues an entire rugby pitch was washed away a few years ago.

Which brings me neatly to the interruptions to my gardening. You can't really concentrate on thinning your Little Gems when in Paris *L'Equipe du Chardon* – the Team of the Thistle – is about to enter the magnificent Stade de France and thousands of tartan-clad, St Andrew's cross-daubed sons and daughters of Caledonia will roar out *O Flower of Scotland*. So I abandon my lettuces, trudge back down the hill, ease off my boots, hang up my straw hat by the hole in the brim, settle down in front of the television to hold my breath for 80 minutes, and will the thin dark-blue line to hold and the fire and dash of the Scottish XV to roll back the French as triumphantly as the charging Scots Greys rolled up Napoleon's columns at Waterloo.

The Languedoc is the heartland of French rugby. I hadn't really thought much about it until one day, shortly after arriving in France, a burly, feisty, gravel-voiced man we'd sometimes seen about Bardou thrust his hand out to me and said, with a kind of conspiratorial leer that was almost propositional, '*Meerayfeel!*'

Meerayfeel? I groped desperately for the slightest clue. Was this a greeting in Occitan, in the *patois*? Was it perhaps a proposition?

'*Meerayfeel!*' he said again. '*Shalmair! Gaveenasteeng! Zhefrees!*' Light suddenly dawned, the beautiful, crisp, clear light of joyous comprehension. He'd probably exhausted all he knew about Scotland: Murrayfield, the Scottish national rugby ground; Chalmers, Gavin Hastings, Jeffrey (with a final S for some reason), great players from a great era in Scottish rugby. To quote *O Flower of Scotland*, when will we see their like again?

I replied in kind, with a few great names of the early 90s ('Parc des Princes! Sella! Cambérabéro!'), the ice was broken and a few weeks later the man I got to know as Francis invited us to watch a France v. Scotland match on his television, the only one in the village.

The jaw trembled and the eye smarted with raw emotion as *O Flower of Scotland* shook the mild air of a sunny February afternoon, at least for us outside: Francis' house wasn't much bigger than a broom cupboard, although it went up three floors. Once he and Ginou and their prop-forward-sized son Christophe were installed there wasn't room for anyone else, so his guests had to perch on kitchen stools in the lane outside and peer in through the open window.

No such problem in Olargues. It's the last tournament of the 1900s, the last before Italy joins the five founder members to make it *Les Six Nations*: the referee whistles the start of the last France v. Scotland clash of the century.

An early French try, and the commentators, including the veteran *rugbyman* Albaladéjo, are cock-a-hoop. A one-a-minute series of crushing Scottish tries alters the balance, and presently the commentators are reduced to inconsequential chit-chat, not always quite on the ball: after much discussion, they agree that the Scottish forward Bulloch's name is pronounced 'blosh', and that Scottish rugby has no more dedicated supporter than Princess Anne, the Queen's sister. Finally, a full 20 minutes from the end, Albaladéjo admits defeat. *On ne peut plus gagner*, he says quietly, we can no longer win. Does he know that, curiously, the signature tune of French rugby on television is an aria from Handel's opera *Rinaldo*, sung by as full-throated a mezzo as Theodora Ciucur? *Lascia, ch'io pianga*, leave me to weep. For once it's well chosen.

Back in the *potager*, thrilled and excited, I feel drawn to celebrate a thumping Scottish victory, and I cast about for something commemorative to plant. Peas, carrots, potatoes, onions, lettuces, radishes, they'll all grow here just as readily as north of the Border. But a visit to a local nurseryman to buy strawberry plants shows me, unexpectedly, the very thing: what grows in every kitchen garden in Scotland, but which you never see in the Midi?

So we leave the nurseryman with a modest pot-grown stand of rhubarb. Battered straw hat on again, I prepare the ground, digging it deep, removing any roots, stones, grubs and other foreign bodies which could possibly interfere with the well-being of the festal, celebratory rhubarb. I'm on the point of lovingly, tenderly easing the slender red stems and familiar dark green leaves out of the plastic pot when there's another interruption, from Wembley this time, temporary home to Welsh rugby while their Millennium stadium is being completed in Cardiff. Down tools, switch on the television again, gasp unbelievingly as at the very last moment Wales beats England by a single point, denying them the championship and allowing Scotland to win the last-ever Five Nations Tournament. Ecstasy.

'*Cela est bien joué,*' as Candide might have said, '*mais il faut cultiver notre jardin.*' Exactly so, rhubarb and all.

Consumed With Moderation

The bus would have left St Pons punctually at 9am if the President and the Vice-President had been on time. Everyone else was there, all fifty sopranos, altos, tenors and basses, plus Serge the driver, standing in little knots in the January sunshine, tapping watches and muttering *mince, alors!* in disapproval.

Eventually the miscreant office-bearers turned up. Monique, the President, rarely lets the mini-whirlwind of busy-ness she trails behind her disturb her *chic* elegance, but this Sunday morning she was ruffled. She'd gone to collect the VP from an outlying village and had found her still in bed. Let no one think she didn't know her Presidential duty, she scolded the *mince alors* merchants: if anyone had remarks to make, let them be addressed to the VP on account of her scandalous inability to get up in the morning. But it's difficult to recriminate when the tousled and sleep-ridden delinquent comes amongst you for *la bise*, and at 9.15 Serge's green and white bus headed south for Berlou.

You've never heard of Berlou? It's not surprising. Berlou is an obscure village tucked away in a hidden fold of the endless Languedoc vineyards. Wait, though: could there be an unsuspected Berlou presence in your local store or supermarket? Next time you glumly push your trolley down the aisles, look for a wine labelled St Chinian, and the chances are that it started its charmed life on the vine-clad slopes around Berlou. Stop a moment, cheer up, smile, dream of beakers-ful of the warm South with beaded bubbles winking at the brim, of the sun and the song of the cicada and the scent of wild thyme; and just to complete the full flavour of the Midi, I'd better add the usual French government health warning: *L'abus d'alcool est dangereux. A consommer avec modération.* Acohol abuse is dangerous. To be consumed with moderation.

Local pundits reckon that Berlou is the best of the St Chinian reds, and there's a strong case to be made for it. Preferably in wood, embossed and printed Berloup (there's a curious regulation forbidding the conventional spelling of the village of origin on the label) and carrying the usual production credits: *Conditionné* (prepared and matured) by So-and-so, *Embouteillé* (bottled) by Such-and-such, and, after our outing in Serge's bus, *Etrenné* (handselled) by the St Pons choir. No choir could ever have had a pleasanter mission than to celebrate St Vincent's day, patron saint of the Berlou wine producers.

Even the winding country road to Berlou was decorated in honour of St Vincent, road signs hidden beneath swags of mimosa blossom and telegraph poles decked with wreaths of bay glistening in the sun. In the tiny church, our destination, an enormous plastic bunch of grapes hung reverently over an altar laden with about seventy bottles offered for dedication by the local *producteurs*. The labels were bright and brash, irregularly lettered and decorated with bunches of grapes and childish figures busy with various local activities, playing football or *boules*, hoeing, sunbathing, cycling: the Berlou primary school children had been roped in to do their bit for a community effort.

Crammed into a tiny side-chapel we rehearsed all the sung items of the Mass, *Kyrie*, *Gloria*, and so on, and finally we ran through an energetic hymn in praise of wine called *Coupo Santo*, Hallowed Cup in Occitan, the ancient language which country people revert to in matters concerning their roots. After a short break the *maire* of Berlou led a service-opening procession, which took a sudden lurch back in time as the *Confrèrie*, the local Guild of wine-producers, advanced majestically down the aisle, a dozen men in traditional costume, the plumes of their three-cornered hats nodding, brilliant red cloaks brushing the ancient flagstones and gold chains of office jingling. Two splendidly-robed priests brought up the rear: one was to distinguish himself later with an enthusiastic retelling of the water-into-wine miracle at Cana of Galilee.

After a short sermon in praise of God revealed in nature – and nature in Berlou consists largely of acres and acres of neatly trimmed vineyards – the choir sang the *Coupo Santo* with fire and gusto. Odd lines show that it's a hymn celebrating a deeply-rooted people and its bards:

D'un vièi pople fièr e libre . . .

(Of an ancient people, proud and free)

Per la glôri dóu terraire . . .

(For the glory of the homeland)

Lou vin pur de noste plant . . .

(The pure wine of our vineyard)

E, se toumboun li felibre, toumbara noste nacioun.

(And, if the poets fall, our nation will collapse)

Vuejo-nous la Pouësio, per canta tout ço que viéu Car es, elo, l'ambrousio que tremudo l'ome en diéu.

(Let us drink to Poetry, to celebrate everything that lives, because that's the ambrosia that changes man into god.)

You could be forgiven for imagining that the *Coupo Santo* has its roots as far back in the past as the people it was written for, and it comes as a surprise to learn that the words are by Frédéric Mistral, the Provençal *félibre* or poet, who won the Nobel prize for literature in 1904, but not necessarily for this poem.

We sang it again at the reception afterwards in the *salle polyvalente*, the village hall. We walked down from the church, glad of the sun on our backs after the January chill of an unheated church. Curiously, the ground outside the hall was strewn with yellow grains of maize. Another local custom, we wondered, maybe to propitiate the spirits of maize-hungry wild boar, which sometimes ravage vineyards, tearing the ripe trusses from the vines?

We suggested this to the VP, now restored to favour in the atmosphere of sunny *bonhomie*. She looked at us as though our imaginations had had one over the eight, as though we'd failed to *consommer avec modération*. No, she said, scornfully: last night there'd been *loto* (bingo) in the hall and as usual the players placed maize grains on their cards to mark called numbers. That way one could use the cards again and again. We were looking at the hall-cleaner's sweepings, nothing more.

Mince alors.

If a bottle of Berlou ever finds it way into your shopping trolley, think of the traditions and pride that go into making wine down here. Dream of the sun, the music, the heady scent of mimosa, the goodwill, if you like. *Avec modération*, of course. Cheers! – or, as they say in Occitan, *a la bona vostra!*

Bon Courage, Monsieur Le Président

There wasn't much of a commotion, really. We heard a few car horns in Labastide, a couple of kilometres away down in the valley, and the peace of a perfect May evening trembled for a few moments. Nothing much – two or three cars, maybe, driving the length of the Boulevard Carnot and back, hand firmly on the horn.

A few disappointed Castres Olympique supporters returning from

Paris, we wondered? Castres Olympique had been defeated the evening before in the final of the French rugby club championships. Castres, a fine town half-an-hour west of Labastide, is very much the local team: many windows and balconies sport blue and white favours whenever Castres is to the fore.

A wedding, maybe? Surely not. The hooting was too half-hearted for the traditional cavalcade of 20 or 30 cars tooting joyously all the way from the Mairie to the church or the reception. Besides, it was Sunday, not a usual day for weddings.

Then we realised. There was a sort of wedding, as it turned out, which explained the car horns: after 14 years of courtship, Marianne finally said *oui* to Jacques Chirac as President of France, and the Labastide car horns, however mutedly, were celebrating his electoral success. This isn't Chirac country; there weren't any fireworks or dancing in the streets in an area traditionally left-wing. We turned the radio on, impressed by the speed of the election results, just in time to hear his chief rival, Lionel Jospin, gracefully and courteously conceding victory. The Languedoc would have liked to see Jospin win, not only as a socialist but as a teacher from near Toulouse, the regional centre the western Languedoc leans towards.

You wouldn't have thought anyone bothered much about politics here, certainly not with extremes of left or right, amid the rolling herb-scented Languedoc hills or the vineyard-covered Mediterranean plain, dotted with sun-drowsy villages. There are so many better things to do, like taking an unhurried two-hour lunch followed by a quiet siesta in the shade of the mulberry tree, or finding an evening game of *boules* in the Place de la République quite enough to soak up your ideological combativeness.

And yet: the surface of French life seems sunny and uncomplicated, but mention politics to a man like César Desjoyeaux, by no means a one man band, and you plumb dark and turbulent depths of the French soul, stirring up angry discontent or despairing incomprehension. It's the Western *malaise*: social spending growing ever faster than the means to pay for it. Strikes and all the paraphernalia of making an intolerable nuisance of yourself until your grievances are met, why, say the socialistically inclined, this is dialogue, this is dialectic, this is the very stuff of consensus politics. Oh! say others, more inclined to the right, if only we'd had your Madame Thatcher! She'd have sorted them out! Anxious not to get caught in the crossfire, I nail my political colours firmly to the fence. In any case, we expats don't have the right to vote in presidential elections, so what we think is academic anyway.

Lack of a vote didn't prevent us from receiving the same electoral material as everyone else. There wasn't much: M. Robert, the Labastide postman, only had two pamphlets to deliver. The first, from Jacques Chirac, outlined his plans for leading France into the 21st century. It was authoritative and well-argued for positive change, especially in the field of unemployment. There were photographs of him in the company of Helmut Kohl, Bill Clinton and John Major, now all passed from the world political scene in varying degrees of oblivion, and I suppose this choice of associates said as much about him as any of the text.

The second pamphlet was from Jean-Marie Le Pen and his National Front party. Le Pen seemed to stand for France for the French and for sending everyone else home, or somewhere else, anyway. That was the way to solve unemployment, that and punitive taxes on imports. His attitude to Europe, which most concerned us because we draw our right to live in France from our citizenship of the European Union, was at the least enigmatic. Le Pen's photographic associates were a curious pair: he was shown in audience – separately – with King Hassan of Morocco and the Pope.

A few years later Le Pen was to give a violent but short-lived shake to the political apple tree, but on this occasion he got no further than the first of two rounds of voting, so it's hardly worth analysing his choice of photographic sponsors. Nor need we waste time delving into why his pamphlet featured so many blonde, blue-eyed folk in his vision of

France under his presidency. All the same Le Pen did very well in Mediterranean France, Provence and the Languedoc.

This was slightly alarming, as though the cattle trucks were already in the sidings in Narbonne ready to cart off the local non-French population. Improbable as it seems, the local Communist vote was high too, so those same cattle trucks might have been ready to start for the Gulags if the Communist leader Robert Hue had made it to the Elysée palace. Even in Labastide, Labastide of the Chirac car horns, the PCF – *Partie Communiste Française* – has a strong presence, although, in the persisting sense of betrayal by the collapse of Moscow-dominated communism, maybe a faltering one. For years the *Bastidiens*, the citizens of Labastide, were treated to a running down-with-this, down-with-that commentary from a local luminary of the PCF, who owned a shed with its back wall facing on to the main street, the Boulevard Carnot. He kept this wall brilliantly white, the better to paint bright red hammers and sickles and PCF slogans on.

Shortly after the presidential election *60% DES FRANÇAIS N'ONT PAS VOTÉ POUR CHIRAC* (60% of the French population did not vote for Chirac) appeared on the communist wall, at about the same time as a local entrepreneur bought the property next door to convert into a factory making elements for floor and ceiling heating. Unemployment is high in Labastide, a depressed little town doing its best to pull itself up by its boot-straps, and the prospect of jobs was welcomed. However, red-hot slogans next door wouldn't do much for the company's image, so the *maire* of Labastide was consulted to see what could be done. Nobody knows what deal was struck, but the wall has stayed pristine white ever since.

So maybe there wasn't much to fear either from the PCF or the National Front. The voting system allows for the weeding out of maverick or extreme candidates in the first round, leaving the real decision for the second. Just as well: the President of France has sweeping powers, General de Gaulle's legacy, greater than any other European head of state.

Maybe they've got it right in other ways, too. Opinion polls are banned the week before polling, always on a Sunday. The local Mairie becomes the polling station, and the ballot box is placed in full view of the plaster bust of Marianne, decorated with a tricolour sash. I don't know how César Desjoyeaux voted: I doubt if he wavered from his usual deliberate abstention. And if he looked Marianne in the eye, I shouldn't be surprised if she didn't wink at him.

Tears For A Princess

Naturally enough, when the phone rings at 6.40 on a Sunday morning, you suspect either a wrong number or bad news.

In the event it was Mme Maurel, an elderly lady of some standing (she is the widow of a *Procureur de la République*, a very senior public prosecutor), who rang to express her *condoléances*: a poor sleeper, she'd heard the news from Paris at 4am, but had waited until a reasonably civilised hour before picking up the phone.

She broke the news of the car accident in which Diana, Princess of Wales, almost universally known here as Lady Di, had been killed. She'd been so moved that she'd felt impelled to offer her sympathy to the nearest Brit known to her.

The television was switched on. It was true. French television, lacking material at that early hour, was doing its best. One or two people in still-dark London expressed their disbelief, then their sense of loss and tragedy. Others were filmed laying the first flowers against the railings of Buckingham Palace. It was strange to hear French voice-overs covering the first halting, uncertain tributes in English; it was curiously moving, an unexpected jerking back to one's roots, as *La Une*, French TV's first channel, relayed the BBC's solemn, muted version of the National Anthem against a slowly-blowing Union Jack, followed by a news presenter, only vaguely familiar after years of absence from the UK, announcing the death of the princess.

Despite the dearth of material, the French presenter did well, cutting between the BBC coverage and the dawn-tousled Isabelle Baillancourt, *La Une*'s London correspondent, predicting uncertainly what the response from Balmoral or Downing Street might be. Hastily cobbled archive material – happy, still unclouded images of that fairy-tale princess we all gathered affectionately into our national consciousness – contrasted violently with hours-old footage of that appalling accident in central Paris, just by the Pont de l'Alma.

The Pont de l'Alma! A name significant enough in itself: one of the most handsome of the bridges over the Seine, it commemorates a battle in the Crimean War where French and British troops co-operated to pull off a stunning, against-all-odds victory. That Sunday morning, too, Franco-British sympathy was alive and well, and I think the French felt more for Britain than maybe Britain felt for itself. They really took Lady Di to themselves, along with other ikons like Caroline and Stéphanie, the princesses from Monaco. They all formed part of a living, breathing *feuilleton*, an Olympian soap opera in a country which, having denied itself a royal family for 130 years, has to make do with imported role models.

Lady Di in all her modes was probably bigger and more consistent news here than in the UK, to the point where sometimes the French seemed obsessed with her and her doings: how natural that they should assume that all Britain should feel the sense of loss even more sharply. In tiny Bardou, the women (the men of the village, apart from myself and Francis, were away hunting) almost fell over themselves to commiserate. Josie, up for the weekend from Béziers, was in tears. Ginou, her sister-in-law, mourned for the motherless princes, and Thérèse, as shrewd as ever for all her 86 years, had harsh things to say about the press fouling its own wells, though the terms she used were much more robust.

But for me the most poignant reaction came from Francis, the non-hunting retired railwayman, the communist from Narbonne, a man you might suppose quite indifferent to the fate of the privileged, but I think he had a secret soft spot for princesses. Once he invited me into his sanctum at the top of his house in Narbonne, which lay in a street named differently on each side, so that the even numbers were in rue Armand Fallières and the odd numbers in rue Cherche-Midi, or some such names. His house was so old that you could see Roman masonry in his *cave*, but there was nothing antique about the top floor, which he'd turned into his private cinema with the widest-screen television I'd yet seen. The walls were lined with video cassettes of hundreds of rugby matches interspersed with gung-ho, macho films and, tucked away in a corner away from fellow-travelling eyes, the complete *Sissi*.

Sissi is a continental soap about the Empress Elizabeth, wife of Kaiser Franz-Josef, a famous beauty of her time, who met a violent end in Geneva in 1898. The storylines are punctuated with Viennese waltzes, dashing hussar officers, low-cut ball-gowns, hot-house flowers and more than a dash of Ruritania and court intrigue. Could the parallels be more obvious?

That Sunday morning Francis felt he had to pass on the news to his temporary neighbour Ranald, a UK university professor on holiday in Bardou; after all, title or no title, the Princess of Wales was an Englishwoman, a mother and a compatriot, and at the very least a person with a capacity to ease what she could of the world's ills in her own individual way. So he tapped on Ranald's door and loosed forth the news in a torrent of gravel-voiced French, rich in the Midi vowel-sounds and idioms for which Ranald's mostly forgotten school French had done little to prepare him.

Although we're unlikely to know what *Sissi*-based agenda actuated him privately, Francis poured out his tale of the tragic events in Paris surrounding *Laddy Dee*, as millions of French pronounced Lady Di. Ranald listened uncertainly, nodding and saying *oui* in what seemed to be the right places. When it appeared that Francis had finished he said *merci, Monsieur* and shut the door, mystified. He hadn't understood a single word.

Francis lit another Gauloise and trotted home, pleased to have made contact, pleased to have built a bridge between people, between railwayman and professor, between Frenchman and Brit. Would Lady Di have agreed? I'm sure she would, maybe smiling at the story of Francis with that shy, enigmatic smile that captivated so many people in France, even avowed republicans like Francis.

Feu De Joie

It was the sort of silence you could hear. There was nothing, no traffic, no children playing, no car doors slamming in the village half a mile away, no distant strimmers, no garden pumps taking river water, nothing. Just silence. France had come to a halt. The entire country, it seemed, was glued to the television screen.

We were, too, like everyone else in Olargues. It was too fine a summer evening to be indoors, so we watched from the *terrasse* – the paved court beneath the fig tree – through the open French windows. Distant shades of watching international rugby 6 years before with Francis in Bardou! – but this time there was a slightly different sense of being on the outside looking in: any British interest in the football World Cup had long since vanished, so there were no nationalistic hackles to rise, either in joy or frustration. It didn't matter to us too much who won, France or Brazil.

With France's first goal the silence grew momentarily deeper, and then suddenly there came an outburst of distant cheering, a short fanfare of car horns and firecracker bangs from somewhere down in the village. Or were they shots?

A second goal. More cheering, more horns.

A third goal, just before the final whistle, and France had won the World Cup.

We'd been down in the village that morning. It was like wandering about backstage in that dead time before the show opens: everything's ready, all's in place, everyone's set to go, and there's just a boring wait until curtain-up. Still, discussion was lively in the baker's, where an enormous cake in the shape of a football ground was on display, with sugar-paste stands and little marzipan hoardings advertising local businesses, the Bar Funambule, Santucci the builder, Café Laissac, and so on. At the counter Mme Dumont, sparrow-like *doyenne* of the village choir and gymnastic club, was certain France was going to win. It was only fair: Brazil had won so often before, it was somebody else's turn.

At the Café Laissac, headquarters of the Olargues football club, *le patron* was scarlet from the effort of blowing up tricolour clusters of balloons to hang from the plane trees shading his *terrasse*. 'Celebrating already?' we asked. 'It isn't too soon?' By no means, he answered. France was going to win. Absolutely no doubt of it. Hadn't we seen the *Midi Libre*, the local paper? They were sure of it, too. He'd bring it out to us with our coffee. Two *grands crèmes*, wasn't it?

Midi Libre scored an early goal with a prominent article about Fabien Barthez, the shaven-headed French goalkeeper, due to take the field in Paris that evening. We knew Barthez, or Barthès in its alternative spelling, was a local name, but we didn't know Fabien Barthez' grandmother lived near Béziers. Granny Barthez had obviously rummaged in drawers or behind the clock at the bidding of *Midi Libre* and had come up with a photo of Fabien and his sister when they were children of 7 or 8. One up to *Midi Libre*.

After the match all purgatory broke out, shouting, chanting, frantic blowing of car horns, firecrackers, as wild a racket as the silence had been deep during the match. We strolled down to the village in the moonlight to watch all Olargues, a microcosm of France, make merry.

They were very good at it, celebrating a wonderful success with all the fervid individuality you might expect of a nation which boasts, as General de Gaulle once remarked, though I imagine in a different context, 246 different cheeses.

Someone was loosing off signal rockets from the village *boules* pitch, just over the road from the Café Laissac, where, true to the forecast of *le patron*, an ecstatic throng of red, white and blue face-painted figures heaved and chanted. We moved on to Le Funambule (the word means 'tight-rope') to see what was afoot there, but things were much quieter: the summer clientèle is mainly foreign, Dutch and German tourists.

A car surged past, lights flashing, horn blaring in rhythm to the occupants shouting in unison *on a gagné!* We've won! through the open car windows. Another car, draped with tricolours like a giant moth, flashed past on the first of hundreds of hooting circuits of the village. Back at the Café Laissac, they were busy cramming into a car festooned with balloons wrenched from the trees and flags as many bare-chested, tricolour-daubed sons of Gaul as would fit through the sun roof. A blonde-dyed lad shook me gravely by the hand and invited our comments with the careful earnestness of one only slightly sober. *Bravo, la France. Chapeau!* we said. What else was there to say? *Oui*, he agreed, nodding pensively. *On est les premiers. On est champions du monde.* The car roared off in mid-nod to roust them up at Le Funambule, beating out the chant *ILS sont OÙ, les BRÉ-sil-IENS?* (pronounced *brésiliengs* in the Midi fashion): Where are they, the Brazilians?

We strolled back, leaving the village to throb until dawn and later, reflecting, with that insight into human affairs that a *pastis* at the Café Laissac brings, that nations sometimes need fillips like winning the World Cup to sharpen their sense of well-being and self-esteem; the tensions that sometimes rack France would be forgotten and a not always very united country would suddenly seem at one with itself. But for how long?

Well . . . in one Olargues household, a mere half-hour. When Zidane's first goal slipped in in the 28th minute, Maurice Santucci the builder registered his delight by grabbing his heaviest hunting shotgun and firing a volley out of the window. His wife Charlotte had only just got the children off to sleep, never easy on humid summer nights. The storm that broke over his head . . . well, only Brazil fared worse that night.

France's reign as world football champions lasted just four years. At the following World Cup the team took an unexpectedly early flight home, bowing out, as one confused commentator put it, with heads held high. No small-arms fire has been heard chez Maurice lately, but maybe that hasn't got much to do with France's football fortunes: in between World Cups he was elected a local councillor, and new local councillors are all too apt to shrug off their joyful spontaneity and cloak themselves instead in dull dependability. More's the pity. Besides, his girls are growing up now and don't need much rocking to get them off to sleep.

CHRISTMAS

Ap-pie Kriss-masse, Évry-ouane

The posters, bright red for Christmas, have been in every shop window in Labastide for most of December: *Concert de Noël*, presented by La Chorale du Pays de Thomières, to be given in Labastide church.

There's no excuse for not knowing about the Christmas concert. The posters are everywhere, in Marché d'Oc, the *superette* or mini-supermarket, in M. Gasc's pharmacy, in La Poste, in M. Pigassou's bi-weekly wine shop, in the Bar du Centre, in the lovely Patricia's *boulangerie*, in M. Benoist's insurance agency, in the Garage Affre, everywhere. The choir members who have given up their time to go round cajoling shopkeepers to put posters in their windows have reached saturation. They deserve to have a good audience for this alone. They've been practising for this concert, on and off, since the previous February. They've met every Tuesday night in a dusty vaulted cellar beneath the old court-house in St Pons, where some pro-Arab graffiti-ist sprayed *Irak vaincra* (Iraq will win) at the time of Gulf War and the municipal cleansing services haven't quite got round to cleaning it off yet.

Anyway, we're almost ready. We've brought Vivaldi's *Gloria* to a state where it will hang together, and for us it's a bold step on to the edges of the big time. It's the first time we've attempted an extended classical choral work. Some of the choir members are uneasy about it. *On n'est pas professionnels* (we aren't professionals), they say, or *C'est pas Paris* (this isn't Paris), hedging against things going wrong. But none of them is as nervous as I am, though I try to keep my air of *sangfroid* and breezy confidence. If it turns out to be *une catastrophe*, it will be me who carries the can as their conductor.

A couple of hours before the concert is due to start we meet in the church, where it's warm and bright. A thoughtful *concierge* has put the heating on for us, and if any of us are shivering it's not because of the cold, although outside the *tramontane* is sweeping down from the High Languedoc plateau, a vicious wind with the scent of snow in it. Well, if it has to blow, let it be the *tramontane*: the other local wind, the *marin*, steams in wet and warm from the Mediterranean, and for some unknown reason makes the choir sing flat. But then, who on earth is going to turn out on such a marrow-chilling night?

Before the audience – if any – starts to arrive we run through bits of the *Gloria*. It isn't a success. The singing is stale and tepid, the place sounds like an echo chamber, they make the same old mistakes, they chatter and fidget while the soloists are rehearsing, they get shouted at, and after a miserable last run-through everyone troops off in a black mood into the vestry to await the start, muttering dark imprecations quite unfit for the ears of the plaster saints and virgins ranged about the church. I comfort myself with the notion that a bad dress rehearsal makes for a good performance, but it's a chancy truism to put one's faith in. Never mind. Perhaps no one will come. We can all go home and put our feet up in front of the fire. Much more sensible.

A little after the appointed time – we have to respect *le petit quart d'heure méditerranéen* – the choir processes in, followed by the organist, the soloists, then by myself. I turn to bow to the audience, and I see the impossible has happened: the church is packed. They're standing shoulder to shoulder at the back and down the sides. The gallery is full. Most unexpected, the broad central aisle is cluttered with zimmers, wheelchairs and even a couple of mobile beds. They've run out of programmes. No turning back. I lift my baton and we attack – it's the only word for it – the *Gloria*.

I should have known, of course. They've never sung it better. Really crisp, mettlesome, joyous singing. And they're smiling, actually smiling. All they needed was a stiff dose of audience. Not a glum face. Wonderful. But where have all these people come from?

After the interval we perform a dozen carols from round Europe. Despite origins in Poland, or Portugal, or Wales, we've furnished French words for them all, except one: *Away in a manger*. The words are too engrained in us, they're almost a part of our genetic make-up: impossible to contemplate it being sung in anything but English. There's a big problem, though. Virtually no one speaks English here, and most are very reluctant to dare the few words and phrases that have stuck after five or six years of learning English in school. Mention the possibility of speaking English and the usual apologetic reply is *on n'est pas doué pour les langues*, we have no gift for languages, but scratch a *Méridional* deep enough and you're likely to find fluency in French, naturally, but in Spanish as well, and, especially among the older people, the *patois* too. It's northern languages, English and particularly German, that the southern tongue finds difficulty getting itself round. We get round the problem of *Away in a manger* in an unusual but effective way, by blanking out the usual words on the sheet music and substituting a bizarre phonetic language known only to the St Pons choir:

> A–ou–aie ine a maine-geurre, no cribe faur a bedd
> Dze lit-elle Lorde Gi–seuss laie da–oune iz souite edd

And so on. Almost a completely different language. The irreverent thought strikes me that James Joyce might have found it useful for *Finnegan's Wake*, but, equally, that as nobody's going to understand the words anyway it doesn't much matter what language we sing it in.

We finish, the last applause dies away, people begin slowly to disperse. One of our sopranos, the iron-willed *directrice* of the Old Peoples' Home, comes to thank me, smiling as though she has a secret, and indeed she has: she has driven virtually her entire flock, staff, helpers and inmates along to the church, as well as insisting that all the local relations come along to look after Grandma too. No wonder the church was packed.

Outside, the wind has dropped. *Bonnes fêtes!* people call to each other as car doors slam and headlights pick up a few stray snowflakes. *Ap-pie Kriss-masse!* someone says to me, daring their English. *Merci, monsieur;* and many of them.

A Christmas Crib

There's something not quite right about it. There's something that jars. No, it's not the oxen and the asses, the three kings, the shepherds, the angels, the holy family, a chubby and oversized baby Jesus lying in the straw, although they don't actually put him there until Christmas morning. It's something else. It'll come to me presently.

The St Pons cathedral Christmas crib is what the Michelin guide might describe as *vaut le détour*, worth turning aside to see, quite something, a much more elaborate *tableau* than you might see in more Anglo-Saxon-inclined churches. The cathedral, which dates very roughly from about the time William the Conqueror might have been thinking what to give his grandchildren for Christmas, has a long vaulted aisle with several side-chapels, and it's one of these that houses the famous crib.

It must take days to construct each Advent. They make the landscape first, rolling Astroturf fields of not really Mediterranean greenery. Then, before they install the stable and its various occupants, they find room for all kinds of little country cameos: foresters at work, someone fishing, children playing tig, goats being milked, smoke rising from winter chimneys. There's sometimes the same kind of thing in Renaissance paintings of the Nativity, where simple country activities underline the human scale of the first Christmas.

In St Pons cathedral you put a coin in the slot and things start to happen: deftly channelled water turns the model mill-wheel, the sky is lit with heavenly radiance, angelic choirs sing and the bells ring, pulled by four 30 centimetre-high plastic stalwarts in polo neck sweaters. Yes, that's it. Of course. It's the bell-ringers that don't quite fit. Where have I seen them before?

Not in the chapel at Les Verreries de Moussans, anyway, where Achille Vidal, honorary crib-maker for the last fifty years, has been at work. It's the giraffe that gives the game away, that points to Achille as someone with a take on Christmas far out of the ordinary. You might have thought that there was nothing new to be said about Christmas, indeed that its changelessness was its strength. Come to Les Verreries de Moussans on Christmas Eve, one of the three times the church is used for services each year, and be prepared to have your mind opened. That giraffe, with its head lowered and thrust through the stable window . . . but wait, that's not all: here's a polar bear, sniffing at the unaccustomed greenery, holly and shiny laurel, round the stable door. And what about the elephant, eyeing up – with one eye, because the other seems to have fallen out – a couple of oxen? And look, there's a monkey on the stable roof.

Achille is there when I go in, sweeping up surplus laurel leaves and wisps of straw. We shake hands, and he asks me what I think. It's not easy to answer. Various theories course through my head. The least idiotic is that Achille is anxious to stress the essential universality of Christmas, that it has the same meaning from pole to equator. From

Greenland's Icy Mountains To India's Coral Strand, as the hymn goes.

It isn't often that you get the chance to discuss the deeper aspects of an artist's work, to crack the crib, so to speak, face to face with him or her, especially a *fauve* or primitive artist like Achille, so I put this thesis to him earnestly. There's a gale of laughter that echoes round the empty church like a Mexican wave. *Ah, non, non, non,* he says, wagging a contradictory finger, it's nothing like that at all: they're his great-grandchildren's soft toys. They've just about grown out of them. They haven't missed them so far: just wait till they see them at Midnight Mass, *quelle blague!* What a joke! He puts in a little teaser every year. It's his trademark, he says. Last year Gaspard, one of the three kings, wore an Olympique Marseille football shirt. Next year . . . but Achille is in two minds about this Christmas, let alone next, he tells me. The blow has fallen. His doctor has forbidden him to sing, because of the strain his gargantuan, *fortissimo* singing puts on his heart. The doctor was quite specific: in no circumstances was Achille to sing *Minuit, chrétiens* (midnight, Christians) at the Midnight Mass. It's a real belter, like *My Way.* Not a tune you can hum: you have to fill your lungs, throw your head back and let rip. Achille must be 80, at least. I can see the doctor's point, but I'm not certain that he can. *Eh bé*, he says, if you've got to go, you might as well go singing . . .

. . . and it's the grim implications of one Lost in Action that lead me along the wayward path that thoughts sometimes take and give me the clue to those St Pons model bell-ringers, firm-jawed, purposeful, set in their plastic expression. Maybe they're exactly what the Conqueror's grandsons wanted in their Christmas stockings: they're Action Men, stripped of their combat gear and Kalashnikovs and given miniature bell-ropes instead. I suppose it's one way of ensuring peace on earth, if only in the Christmas crib, but I hope the St Pons crib-maker never gets wind of Barbie and Ken.

Hotting Up For Christmas

The *tramontane*, the Languedoc version of the more famous *mistral*, has been blowing for days and it may snow in the valley at any time. The mountains that frame the Olargues valley on the northern side are already sparkling with a seasonal dusting of snow over their topmost crags, and The Lady, a skyline formation of peaks, bumps and outcrops that resembles the profile of a sleeping woman, has a diamanté nose, chin and bosom. Claude Lauze, just the man to ask if you want a Christmas tree that smells of the pine forest rather than the Shanghai sweatshops, reports several centimetres of snow at La Salvetat, a granite and slate village up on the high plateau beyond the buttress of our mountains. It's notoriously cold up there.

Muffled figures unwrap themselves cautiously in M. Gosset's *boulangerie*, glad of a few minutes' warm from the ovens, and the talk is of the weather. *C'est la saison*, it's the season, they say, nodding philosophically, and suddenly global warming and greenhouse effects are wiped off the conversational menu. At the Pharmacie Terral there's a stiff demand for cough mixture and cold remedies, and many complain of *angine*, which I used to imagine, with some alarm, meant Angina Pectoris until I discovered it's simply the French for a sore throat, which often masquerades as tonsillitis.

Natalie, our postwoman, zigzags daily down the mountain road from La Salvetat at exactly the same time as an Olargues girl struggles up to La Salvetat to brave the snow in her yellow post van, despite frequent requests for exchange. French bureaucracy has no equal on earth for perpetuating situations like this, but it's not all to Natalie's disadvantage. Many of the houses in and about La Salvetat are holiday homes, closed and untenanted in winter and only opened up in summer, but down in the valley the pickings are much richer when it comes to the annual pre-Christmas distribution of *L'Almanac de La*

Poste, the Post Office calendar. It's the usual way of soliciting a Christmas box: postal staff buy them in at cost price and sell them to everyone on their rounds for whatever people are prepared to give.

L'Almanac has a cover brightly illustrated with scenes to cater for all tastes, mountains, butterflies, yachts, veteran cars, country crafts, kittens and puppies and so on, and Natalie at least lets you choose the cover you want. M. Robert the Labastide postman once simply pushed that year's calendar, one featuring Arab stallions exercising, into my hands without the option. He'd chosen horses, he said, because he knew we were fond of animals. He wasn't entirely wrong, but I wondered what had guided his choice. The only obvious evidence was M. Gonzales' sheep, for which I used to feel few pangs of fondness when they got out or stuck themselves fast in bramble thickets. Natalie, however, spreads out the choice in a fan and we choose sunlit scenes of the Côte d'Azur, to remind us that winter can't go on for ever.

It's an engaging read, pleasantly full of unexpected information. Months and dates, school terms and public holidays, of course, but all the saints' days are included too. There are so many saints in the Catholic calendar that there isn't room for them all, even at the rate of one a day, and some only get a look-in every few years. Some we're used to: *St Patrice* (March 17th) and *St André* (November 30th), but before we can raise an enquiring eyebrow at *St Kévin* (June 3rd), *St Roméo* (February 25th) and *St Habib* (March 27th) we discover Kévin again: he tops *le hit-parade* – a nice drop of Franglais – of boy's names. For girls, Marine comes first. Last, at No. 60, come Cédric and Béatrice. This is followed by a sort of Government Health Warning, advising parents to think twice before giving their children momentarily fashionable names. If you must christen your child Ombeline or Sullivan, give him or her several other names as well, so that the poor kids can have a choice when they grow up. It's almost impossible to change your first name legally in France.

You never know what to expect. Here's a short but comprehensive

Language of Flowers, covering love's many contingencies. First pangs of fondness, first *frisson* of love? Send him/her *primevères*, primroses. Burning passion? A bouquet of phlox or fuchsia tells all. But if the florist's van arrives with *capucines*, nasturtiums, book yourself a single ticket on the slow boat to Madagascar: they mean indifference. The inevitable must follow: chrysanthemums, *amour terminé*.

Turn the page and we're into the meat of *L'Almanac*, street maps of local towns. It would be hard to lose your way about the narrow cobbled streets of Olargues (population 500) unless you'd sunk several *pastis* over the eight at the Café Laissac, but for anyone needing to brave the spider's webs of roads and seething traffic to do Christmas shopping in Béziers, the street maps have fallen straight from *le père Noël's* sleigh.

So, thanks to Natalie, there's no excuse for not being able to find the hypermarket giants, Intermarché, Auchan, E.Leclerc, Géant and so on, which swarm with shoppers at this time of year. There was a time years ago during holidays in France when a visit to the supermarket was larded with novelty and fun. There was hardly any music, for one thing, certainly not the stiff doses of Euro-pop no French shopper can lift hand to shelf without; although I was really quite struck once to hear *Casta Diva* (O Chaste Goddess – of profit?) from Bellini's opera *Norma* murmuring discreetly from the speakers in Intermarché in Figeac, not really the sort of thing to encourage the punters to shop till they drop. A supermarket visit then promised prime contact with real French people, the opportunity to trot out a few well-rehearsed phrases and fill in a few gaps in one's vocabulary. Who would have thought that a kipper was *une bouffie*, or that *WC Canard* turned out to be dear old Toilet Duck?

Not any more. Thirty minutes is about the limit. The scales have fallen from our eyes. And not just from our eyes, but from our ears too: there was a delicious moment in a local Intermarché, where the fuse-boxes could scarcely cope with Christmas lights blazing and Christmas Euro-pop blaring, but where nevertheless they'd hired *un animateur*, a man to be avoided at all costs, a sort of commercial cheer-leader cruising the aisles with his microphone puffing seasonal products and actually accosting shoppers, asking them their names and dull questions like do they know France's chief European export market and if they do (in fact it's Germany) awarding them a voucher for a brace of *WC Canard* at full volume so that everyone can hear about it.

The *animateur* reported for duty about five minutes after we arrived, when afternoon Christmas shopping was already in full swing. He plugged into the loudspeaker circuit and switched on his microphone. It was the last straw: the supermarket was plunged into darkness and the cheer-leader's '*oh putain*' – not a very Christmassy word – trailed away as '*oh put-t-t-a-a-a-i-i-i-n-n*' into a blissful silence.

Yes, Christmas is hotting up, and Natalie was wise to unload her *Almanacs de La Poste* early. As for me, you'll probably find me down in the Café Laissac until things cool down a bit. *Chin*, as they say down here. Cheers!

Endangered Species

New Year was duly seen in at a favourite restaurant, Le Châtaignon, in the next village, St Etienne d'Albagnan. It's run by a husband and wife team, Gilbert and Claudine Laurent, and we're frequent enough customers to have graduated to our own table, one near the fire of vine stumps on a raised hearth with a chimney breast that sweeps up to the rafters. Besides, Gilbert, the *chef de cuisine*, is guitar accompanist to our choir, Le Choeur des Hauts Cantons, and I hope he would as soon place his *chef de choeur* at a distant and uncongenial table as I would hide him behind the basses at a concert. So from the privilege of a fireside table we enjoy the growing hum of animated conversation, gorgeous scents from the haunches of *sanglier* – wild boar – roasting on the spit, the clink of glasses, sudden unexplained bursts of laughter from other tables, children's voices and all the ambience of the traditional family New Year's Eve meal, the *réveillon*.

The menu led off with *foie gras*, served with a modest salad and squares of toast. Somebody – Sydney Smith? – once said his idea of heaven was eating *foie gras* to the sound of trumpets. If Gilbert and Claudine had been asked to lay on a couple of trumpeters to test this engaging notion, I'm sure they would have done their best. They would have come in handy later on, too.

However, the *foie gras* was firm, consistent, exactly the right temperature and so excellently flavoured that there wasn't much of a problem swallowing both it and our northern sensitivities when we're told that *foie gras* is made by force-feeding geese, by stuffing their feed down their gullets through special funnels with a kind of plunger. It's a process called *gavage*, and the result is that the bird's liver swells to such a size that the poor creature can barely waddle up to receive its daily dose. Apparently geese enjoy being force-fed, especially if the feeder tickles and strokes the bird's crop at the same time. This the-fox-enjoys-being-hunted chop logic doesn't cut much ice with animal welfare lobbies in Brussels and elsewhere who have got wind of it, and not before time, as it's a technique the Romans perfected. So we can expect *gavage* to be banned in due course by some astronomically-numbered Euro-directive. Have we eaten our last *foie gras*?

The lobster tails that followed were perfection and gave rise to no gloomy prognostications, unlike the main course, the *sanglier*. Without the village hunt, *la chasse*, there wouldn't have been any, and Gilbert would have had to spit-roast some other meat. But evidently *la chasse* had been in luck the previous weekend, a deal had been struck, and Gilbert himself emerged from the kitchen to carve from the spit, wiping his brow the while against the heat from the fire.

Village *chasses* in this part of the world aren't far removed from

Dad's Army, and many *chasseurs* feel under a pressure which is hardly surprising in view of the appalling accidents that can occur when a lot of elderly men are let loose over tracts of public land, two or three days a week, with high-powered rifles and shotguns. Time was when *la chasse* thought itself lucky to end up with a *sanglier* a month over the 5-month season, but then wily *chasseurs* saw better sport and more *sous* in breeding wild boar in captivity and then releasing them. That was before a Euro-directive sought to control the unrestricted sale of wild pork by requiring a vet to be present at the point of butchery to certify the quality of the meat.

Now there are wild boar everywhere, rootling through vineyards and cherry orchards, churning up the earth and causing great damage. Pierrot's garden in Bardou was a case in point. I rarely need to rotovate our *potager*: the wild boar will do it for me, ploughing up the soil in search of chestnuts.

Far from the days of wild boar being numbered, it's the *chasseurs* who are threatened, by dwindling numbers and pressure groups who want to enjoy public land without stray bullets zinging about their ears every weekend. The season closes in January: have we seen our last *battue*?

Midnight crept up quietly while profiteroles and champagne were served, and watches were tapped to tell Claudine, who runs the front of house at Le Châtaignon, to send in the trumpeters. However, in their absence she sent the *serveuse*, a homely middle-aged waitress in pinny and sensible shoes, to go round the company wishing them *meilleurs voeux* and *bonne année* and giving them *la bise*: better that, I suppose, than having her jump out of a cake. This snowballed until everyone was on their feet, shaking hands and not being quite certain which cheek, left or right, to offer for *la bise*, a conundrum complicated by the company at the next table, which included a sleeping child, who turned out to be Belgian.

Here in the Languedoc the ration of *bises* is two, a quick left-right, but the number increases to three as you move north, and when you reach Brussels, HQ of Euro-conformity, it has gone up to four. It was well into New Year's Day by the time everyone, perfect strangers mostly, had kissed everyone else, not without some confusion: two, three, or four? Left cheek first, or right? And – vexed question – man to man?

At a *réveillon* in Bardou some years before, on the stroke of midnight the women stood up and moved one way round a long rectangular table, exchanging *la bise* with the men going in the opposite direction, a manoeuvre like the Grand Chain in the Eightsome Reel, notorious for someone getting it wrong and messing up the whole movement. Just so. Behind Thérèse (*bise, bise*), Ginou (*bise, bise*) and Josie (*bise, bise*) loomed Pierrot, followed by Francis. Whether they'd peaked too early on the Blanquette de Limoux and neither knew nor cared which direction they were going in, whether they were deliberately spreading confusion, or whether they were simply asserting a Gallic independence wasn't certain, but here they came offering bristly cheeks to all comers. Crisis.

I ducked out scornfully, offering a hand to shake instead, and realised at once from Pierrot's expression what a blinder of *une gaffe* I'd committed. However difficult it is for Anglo-Saxony to take on board, *la bise* between men is an expression of trust, friendship and acceptance. And I'd spurned it. I can feel my toes curling with the embarrassment yet. Reconstructing the wretched business later in the way that one does, I realised what had happened: at the end of the table sat Emilie, far too majestic a figure for any but the most slender to squeeze behind. Pierrot and Francis, themselves no wraiths, had had no choice but to turn the other way.

At Le Châtaignon no *bise*-seeking men came my way, and after coffee we paid and went home with much to ponder. Nothing is constant but flux: only change abideth. The days of *foie gras* seem numbered. And *la chasse*. Even *la bise* provokes uncertainty. And just then, with the Euro round the corner, the very franc's days were numbered.

Heigh ho. Change and decay in all around I see. I suppose we should have been girding our loins for the 21st century. I don't think we're quite ready for the 20th yet.

POT POURRI

Sa Majesté

'You should try everything once,' somebody once said to the composer Sir Arnold Bax, 'except incest and folk-dancing.' For all I know he followed this precept assiduously, and died a happy man. But did he ever sit himself behind the wheel of a 2CV?

It was in the spirit of trying everything once, especially common, everyday experiences particularly associated with France, that I looked for a second-hand 2CV.

It seemed that driving about in the little car that opened up the roads of France to so many people who wouldn't otherwise have had the chance was an important thing to do for anyone anxious, like myself, to dig deep into the French experience. Sitting one evening with the tenors in the St Pons choir, I told my neighbour René about it. He was doubtful: second-hand 2CVs didn't grow on trees. They weren't too easily found.

However, he must have spoken to someone about it, because a couple of evenings later a M. Danjan rang. He'd heard the news: he had an old 2CV he was wanting to sell. Would I be interested? I went to see it one night, after he'd finished work. It was almost dark: not a good time to inspect a used car.

On the other hand, there wasn't much to inspect. The beauty of the 2CV is its extreme simplicity. At the least, M. Danjan's 2CV had grown out of the complexes of adolescence: it dated from 1969. Was this a vintage year for 2CVs? He listed its advantages: a new engine, two spare wheels, 11 months' road tax, *contrôle technique* (the French roadworthiness test, the equivalent of MOT).

Oh yes, and her reputation as *une vedette de film*, a film star.

'A film star?' I asked. An unusual selling point, surely. No second-hand car lot I'd ever seen featured film stars.

'*Mais oui*,' M. Danjan said, and went on to explain that this very car had starred in a recent video about forest fires, compulsory viewing in all schools in the Hérault *département*, which is often fire-swept in summer and occasionally in winter too. M. Danjan should have known: he was a *sapeur forestier*, a forest fireman, and it was he who'd driven his little car for the video.

He patted the driver's door and invited me to look in the gathering gloom at the Hérault *département* logo fixed to it, a design suggesting sea and sun.

'Everyone knows this little *deuch*. She's famous,' he continued. ('*Deuch*' is short for *deux chevaux*, two horses, or 2CV, which really means two horse-power.) 'The police will never stop you. And you can park anywhere you want. A film star's privilege.'

He invited me to try it. It was terrifying. Left-hand drive, naturally, and the first time I'd attempted it. No seat belts, but some primitive kidney-slicing lap restraints instead. All the hand controls the 'wrong' way round, including a spongy push-me-pull-you column gear shift.

No giant, I asked how to move the seat forward. There was a hollow laugh. It was obviously impossible.

We set off on our test drive, myself in a semi-prone position enjoying pleasant views of the St Pons night sky framed between upper storeys and odd glimpses of narrow twisting streets, if they rose steeply enough in front of us. Once I got into second gear, probably by mistake. I don't remember too much about it. An episode best forgotten.

I think I must have bought it out of a determination not to be beaten. It took about three weeks to master it. A firm hand wasn't enough: it had to be bullied. There was no finger-tip control, like the Volvo we'd brought from the UK, no effete luxuries like power assisted braking or steering. No ten-to-two position on the steering wheel, either: you needed both hands to heave and wrench the wheel round, like a man-of-war in a storm.

But gradually the battle was won and the upper hand gained, to the point where it was used for most local journeys. It was noisy: there was no exhaust, just an expansion box under the driver's seat. It was unheated and draughty, although a lot of fun in summer with the canvas roof rolled back. It was inconvenient: the lower half of the front windows hinged upwards and outwards, fastened by a clip that gave way with every jolt. It's common knowledge in France that you can always tell a 2CV driver from his or her bruised and swollen left elbow. It was slow, but I wouldn't have been without it.

It? What am I saying? She, her. Cars are feminine in France. *La* Volvo, *La* Mercedès, *La* Ferrari, *La* Jaguar, *La* deuch. *Oh là là.* You have to respect their femininity . . . and as if in return, there were several agreeable surprises. M. Danjan was right: she did have a magic way of sailing through random police checks. Parking isn't much of a problem in a little town like St Pons. I wouldn't have pushed my luck anyway, *vedette de film* or not.

Even more agreeably surprising was the annual road tax. You buy *vignettes*, self-adhesive road tax discs, from tobacconists – an extraordinary system, typically French – in late November for the following year. The tax is calculated on the car's age and engine size, expressed in horsepower. I took the *carte grise*, the car's registration document, along to M. Maury, who ran a tobacconist's, occultist bookshop and cobbler's just along from the cathedral.

'Ah,' he said, '*Sa Majesté*. Two horse power? 25 years old? At 25 your car becomes a *voiture de collection*, a collector's car, and is tax-exempt. There's nothing to pay, Monsieur.'

Magic words. Better still, her value almost doubled a month or two after buying her: to stimulate new car sales, the government introduced, for a limited period, a guaranteed minimum trade-in for any car able to make it to the garage under its own steam. This scheme may have worked wonders for the French car industry, but it automatically set a minimum, and often inflated, value on every old banger.

But I wasn't interested, not then, anyway. Sell *Sa Majesté*? Unthinkable. It would have been like contemplating incest. Or folk dancing.

A Swarm Of Bs

Our former neighbour Emilie, the majestic old lady who lived in a farmhouse down the lane from Bardou with only her little dog Pompon for company, once gave me a lesson in the colloquial, everyday French that everyone speaks but that you never learn in school or evening class or even at university. All the important things in life, she said, start with B.

She gave me a second or two to think, but I was stumped and gave in. Eyes twinkling with triumph, she began her list. *Baraque*, house; *boulot*, work; *bouffe*, food, eating; *balles*, francs, money; *bringue*, party.

I recognised some when she mentioned them, but then she came out with a new one: *bagnole*, car. It comes out phonetically as 'ban-yoll', a nice word with overtones of disreputable scruffiness, translatable as 'old banger' or even the old-fashioned 'jalopy'.

Exactly right, in fact, for our old Volvo, well into what the French call *le troisième âge*, and like everything approaching the evening of life few things worked as they once did. 160,000 miles on the clock (which raises only a few eyebrows here, as they assume it's kilometres), rust rampant underneath, the legacy of sea mist and winter salt on Scottish roads, an alarming shudder from the clutch: a lot of *boulot* and even more *balles* to put right.

Another vital B, at that time, for anyone in the car trade was *Balladur*, spelt with a capital B because it was the name of a Prime Minister who gave his name to the minimum 5000 francs trade-in scheme we came across with *Sa Majesté*. It worked very well, but it had a fatal flaw: it lasted only as long as its maker remained Prime Minister. French Prime Ministers didn't last very long in the early 90s, but by the time Edouard Balladur handed over the keys of the Palais Matignon to Alain Juppé we'd taken full advantage of it.

Five thousand *balles* guaranteed trade-in came then to about 640 quid, to preserve the colloquial idiom, more than twice the price the poor old Volvo would have fetched in the UK. In addition, there would have been the cost of getting it there. We would have been lucky to clear £50 towards the journey home.

Happy hours were spent toying with various replacements, plaguing car salesmen, test-driving this, almost deciding that, until the choice fell on a Peugeot 306 diesel labelled *faible kilométrage*, low mileage, at Garage Affre down in Labastide. A very satisfactory test drive along the road to St Pons and back, and the decision was made: go for it. But, of course, it wasn't new. No new *bagnole*, no *Balladur*.

French logic, subtly manipulated by M. Bintz (another of Emilie's Bs, perhaps?), the Garage Affre salesman with a taste for those garish kipper ties that went out in Britain in the 80s, came to the rescue. If the front door's locked, try the back door: there was nothing to say the *Balladur* wasn't transferable. He would set the Volvo against someone else's new car, someone without a trade-in. As simple as that. More, he offered 7000 francs as the trade-in price, plus a free *carte grise*, the registration document, which has to be renewed with each change of owner. It's not often a kipper-tied car salesman makes you an offer you can't refuse. How much the someone else knew about it I don't know. M. Bintz moved on somewhere else shortly afterwards. He's probably Prime Minister by now.

So there was an air of finality about the *adieu* made to the old Volvo, last seen looking forlorn in the used car pen at Garage Affre with *Balladur* scrawled in white across the windscreen. RIP. Rust in peace.

And *bonjour*, Peugeot 306. So far, so good. Pleasant, light handling, a nice turn of speed, unbelievable fuel economy after the Volvo (M. Bintz thought we could probably make it to the Channel on one tankful of diesel, and he wasn't far wrong) and, with left-hand drive, no giraffing across the passenger seat to see if it's safe to overtake.

I'm rarely in a hurry, so there won't be too much overtaking, certainly not in the all too common French style, a quick no-signals flip in and out. No, I'll hang on to my British habits, *merci*. Or some of them, anyway: if you're in France this or any summer and someone stops for you at a pedestrian crossing, smile and wave, because it'll be me. I'm virtually the only person in France who does. *Très correct, très britannique.*

But of course *britannique* didn't rate a mention in Emilie's list of Bs.

Perhaps I've been impatient, wanting to push things along faster than they'll bear it, but all the same two years seems a long time to wait for a cat to start earning its keep. Ours always was a particular beast, designed more for ornament than use, ever since I saved it from a watery fate in a friend's bucket and brought it home in the car.

To overcome – I'd better not say drown – its feverish mewlings and clawings inside its cardboard box I put a tape on, Brahms' *Requiem*, but it only squawked the louder, and it was a no-holds-barred live recording of the Ness River Rhythm Kings that eventually lulled it into a moody, uneasy silence. Not an easy journey, not an auspicious beginning.

Two years later people say *Qu'il est beau, ce chat*, what a very fine cat, and well they might seeing the French cat food it gets through. A 4-pack of its 'Caresse' individual Repas du Terroir contains:

> *Fricassée au Porc et aux Lentilles*
> *Cassolette au Thon à la provençale*
> *Gratinée à l'Agneau*
> *Gibelotte au Lapin et aux Pruneaux.*

A poem in itself, like many French menus. You could do worse at Le Châtaignon.

They go on: *Il est français, votre chat?* He's French, your cat? and I think they ask because it's too sleek and well-fed to resemble the scrawny, ill-favoured brutes that pass for cats elsewhere in France. Or maybe they ask to find out which language, French or English, to address it in. It makes no difference, it can't distinguish 'minou' from 'puss' and – apart from the Ness River Rhythm Kings – the only sound it responds to is having its feeding bowl tapped. Even the elemental thunderstorms we sometimes endure, when earth's very foundations tremble, barely ruffle its serene countenance.

In fact, it is different from most French cats. At six months I took him, as he was then, accompanied by *Cakewalkin' Babies Back Home* hot and strong, to M. Govaerts the St Pons vet, who turned him into an it, operation for which he told me there was almost no demand. French friends and neighbours raised their eyebrows at such spendthrift lunacy: for the price, Pierrot would have been delighted to *supprimer* any unwanted kittens our cat might in his way have been delighted to *engendrer* until either the cat, his supply of buckets and flower pots or he himself expired. As usual, when major differences of outlook between Anglo-Saxony and the Midi surface, I say nothing (it saves being misquoted), beam amiably at everyone, move a little further into the sun and invite Pierrot to pour himself another *pastis*.

His dog Diane lives in a tea-chest outside his front door, tethered night and day by a metre of chain. She gets plenty of exercise barking and trying to break free, and when she does occasionally wrench her chain off she wanders about by the door and whines miserably until someone ties her up again. Pierrot draws all sorts of homespun philosophy from a situation which in the UK would invite dawn raids by animal welfare agencies and a few stiff words from the bench: Diane, he says, has never known any different; she's kept clean, well fed and watered, which is quite true, and anyway better chained up than end up, like some dogs allowed to wander, *chez la chintoque*.

Une chintoque is a vulgar expression meaning a Chinese or oriental woman, and Pierrot's disturbing reference is to the rumoured tendency for *fricassée* of stray dog to turn up in Vietnamese restaurants in the area . . .

Returning hurriedly to the cat, a belated inkling of the cooking-pot threat may have reached its ears and caused it to reconsider urgently its whole purpose on this earth, because a little later it seemed desperate to get into the *cave*, the vaulted stone wine cellar, at La Prade Haute.

Wondering why, I let it in and closed the door, so as not to disturb the constant temperature of 9 degrees. Half an hour later our dog Bellamy wanted to go in too. Very strange.

When I finally called time, there was an unusual scene in there, a *tableau* of nature red in tooth and claw. The cat and dog were looking daggers at each other, and equidistant between them lay a newly-dead *loir*, the destructive – not disdaining famous composers' harmoniums, as we've seen – grey and white house squirrel about the size of a guinea-pig with a large fluffy tail. *Loirs* live in the roof and, from the sound of it, hurl rocks at the roof timbers, squeaking ecstatically, in the early hours. Clearly there are secret *loir*-passages, of the sort that used to enthral me as an Enid Blyton-addicted small boy, between the *cave* and the roof.

So I picked the cat up and petted it, said bravo, that was the way, it had been a long wait but it had been worth it, keep up the good work, plenty more where that *loir* came from . . .

What *loir*? It had gone, all but its head and tail, while I was making a fuss of the cat. No need to look far for the culprit, licking her chops and wagging her tail. Poor cat, dispossessed at every turn. *C'est dur, la vie*, as Pierrot would say. Life's hard.

Rab, Marianne And Co

A London paper which we bought in Béziers carried a story about the apparent reluctance of Scotsmen to be seen dead in the male toiletries department of Boots or elsewhere, and gracing the article were the unlovely but endearing features of Rab C. Nesbitt, dark TV star of Scottish satire, whose grunted utterances are so obscure that subtitles have to be added for ease of understanding south of the Border.

The world spun uncertainly for a few seconds, a tangled confrontational whirl of Béziers on a Friday in October (scatter of autumn leaves, sun filtered through the plane trees lining the Allées Paul Riquet, the great central avenue, the colours and scents of the weekly flower market, with no one in much hurry) and this gross, bloody-bandaged, filthy, string-vested image of Scotland.

I fell to wondering: if ever a national competition sought to find somebody representing the essential spirit, the soul, the embodiment and outward face of Scotland, Scotland's equivalent of John Bull or Uncle Sam, how many votes would Rab C. Nesbitt garner?

The essential spirit, the soul, etc., etc. of France is a young woman we've met before: Marianne. Her bust adorns every Mairie, she appears on postage stamps, on government headed notepaper, solicitors' brass plates, passports, tax office rubber stamps, parking tickets, voting cards, anything with a whiff of officialdom. There are statues of her here and there, and everyone knows the most celebrated one, which isn't in France at all but at the entrance to New York Harbour: the Statue of Liberty is really Marianne, a gift from the people of France in 1876 to the USA to mark the centenary of the Declaration of Independence.

It's very seldom that we find ourselves in the right place at the right time, and the nearby town of St Pons is such a sleepy little place that you wouldn't think anything ever happened there to be in time for. However, St Pons has a 3-metre statue of Marianne, painted green and with torch held aloft. She used to stand on a plinth of red-veined local marble in the middle of the cathedral square, lapped by market stalls on Wednesdays and by *boules* players and parked cars on other days. I write 'used to', because Marianne isn't there any longer. She's gone on her travels. Not very far, just across the road, in fact, to the marble-paved court in front of the Mairie.

Going to St Pons to pay the rates, we arrived by coincidence to find Marianne, green no longer but sandblasted down to her original bronze, dangling on the end of a crane and swinging slightly in the breeze. She'd just completed her 50-metre journey and was hovering a few centimetres above her new plinth, waiting for her final lowering. It was clearly An Occasion.

They'd put a rough decking round the top of the plinth, and queues of St Pons schoolchildren were waiting to climb up, class by class, to be photographed with the *maire*, Kléber Mesquida, a commanding figure in dark suit and tricolour sash, all smiles: at least, the smiles persisted until Marianne's breeze-assisted pendulum-like swing threatened an early by-election. The classes seemed never-ending, M. Mesquida's smile thinned into a worried frown, and he was heard to shout down to a group of carefree, fag-in-mouth councillors '*Mon dieu,* how many more of them are there?' We rather suspected that the children were enjoying it so much that once they'd climbed down they joined the end of the queue for another go.

We recognised several old friends and acquaintances among the St Pons citizens gathered for The Occasion: Gabriel Rodriguez the museum curator; Claire Granier, who runs the Maison de la Culture et de la Jeunesse, the Youth and Culture Centre, not always a happy mix; Josie Auzias, head of the Catholic primary school, surrounded by her flock and offering her cheek for *la bise*. It's a fine thing to be able to kiss a working headmistress in broad daylight, not the sort of thing that comes anyone's way in Scotland, not even Rab C. Nesbitt's, but clearly this is one of the liberties Marianne presides over.

We paid the rates and left them to it. The next time we passed the Mairie, Marianne, a generously endowed lady, and muscular enough to hold high the flaming torch of French culture well into the next millenium, had been firmly bolted to her plinth and M. Mesquida had come through unscathed.

In the 1960s someone had the bright idea of having a living, breathing Frenchwoman to model the Personification of France. There was one obvious candidate for Marianne at that time, Brigitte Bardot, the sultry star of *And God Created Woman*, so BB's head, slightly stylised, adorned postage stamps and mayors' parlours for 20 years, until she was replaced by Catherine Deneuve. Now the *maires* of France's thousands of *communes* have voted for a Marianne to start the third millenium off, and an elegant, willowy Corsican actress called Laetitia Casta topped the poll.

That she later went to live in England protesting about the level of French taxes hardly seems to matter now. And who knows? One day an elegant, willowy statue of Marianne, a gift to the Scots from the French, may grace the frontier at Gretna Green or Coldstream. And if she's portrayed wearing a string vest, you'll know who's been at work.

Reading Between The Lines

We pick up a copy of *L'Echo des Hauts Cantons* every fortnight. It's a local freesheet, one you help yourself to in the shops. Maybe the title needs explaining: *L'Echo* speaks for itself, but the *Hauts Cantons* points to the scattered hill villages and impenetrable valley settlements of the country between the Haut and Bas Languedoc. Our country, in fact.

If you've got nothing better to do for a few moments, close your eyes . . . switch on the sun, clothe the hillsides with oak and chestnut forests, patchwork every flattish piece of land with terraced vineyards, olive groves and cherry orchards, fill your nostrils with scents of wild thyme and your ears with distant church bells and the whirring of crickets, and you're here. In fact, you could be just about to pick up your copy of *L'Echo* from the Tustabouïsse village shop – but I'm jumping the gun.

There's never any news in *L'Echo*. News travels much faster through rural communities than printing it in a fortnightly freesheet could ever achieve. Besides, the Béziers edition of *Midi Libre* has a daily page devoted to local ongoings. You use *L'Echo* if you've got something to sell. It's full of small advertisements, the sort that really give you a feel for the local economy and what makes the people of the Hauts Cantons tick.

A late August edition gives a rich haul. The hunting season has just started, a fortnight earlier than usual because of the dramatic increase of wild boar just at the time when the grapes hang heavy on the vines, at exactly the right height for sharp tusks and bristly snouts to start their own nocturnal grape harvest, so the columns of *L'Echo* hang equally heavy with adverts for hunting dogs.

Here, for instance, is someone selling Jagdterrier puppies, excellent hunting pedigree, while someone else has Khortal bitch puppies on offer, born in June to *parents bécassiers*, woodcock retrievers. Khortal is an unfamiliar breed to me, and I can't say that Teckel, Briquet, Beauceron or Gascon Blue turn up very frequently in the UK either. In fact I'm surprised that they mention breeds at all. Most of the hunting dogs in the area are such a scruffy Heinz 57 rag, tag and bobtail as to strike terror into the heart of any wild boar, itself no oil painting, by their fearsome looks alone. Maybe it's a hunting mongrel that the next advertiser has for sale, a 7-year-old bitch *extra* (colloquial French for wonderful, almost miraculous) for putting up and retrieving hares, rabbits and pheasants but *nul* (useless) for deer. *Possible essai*, try her, it goes on, in the shorthand of small ads, as though the seller was offering a test run in a second hand car.

It's just possible that the person selling his *extra* bitch is none other than Tabot. Tabot's adventures – apocryphal, of course – provide the only editorial in *L'Echo*. Apparently his column is very popular. He's the archetypal beret-wearing, blue-overalled French peasant, a rural philosopher and a keen observer of life in Tustabouïsse (a village not to be found on any map, but not far from any village you've ever known) as he hoes his onions and pours his lunch-time *pastis*. His tales of *la France profonde*, of Deepest France, show that he's at the centre of village life with its occasional triumphs and many disasters: mini-disasters would be better, because no one gets seriously hurt. There's a

P.G. Wodehouse-like timelessness about his world: *sangliers* ravage gardens (shades of Pierrot's garden in Bardou!), Baptiste's goat savages the postman, a sudden gust sends Le Tienot's beach umbrella nosediving into some holidaying Germans' picnic. But Tabot plays by the rules, causes no trouble and nothing is ever his fault. Arguably Tabot is France.

But there's another reason for his popularity. His column, *Le Recoin du Tabot*, Tabot's Corner, appears twice, first in standard French and then in Occitan, the descendant of low Latin that's still spoken widely in the Midi, although its more dominant cousin is slowly doing it to death. Every fortnight I turn straight from *Le Recoin du Tabot* to read the same story again when it resurfaces a few pages later in Occitan as *Lou Recantou del Tabot*. Or try to read it: I get on about as well with Occitan as Joyce does with French, which isn't saying much.

Joyce? Tabot's adventures wouldn't have anything like the same *panache* to them without Joyce. She's an expat Brit, with strong American connections, who's chosen to live in Tustabouïsse. Tabot fancies Joyce. What red-blooded Frenchman wouldn't? She comes from the same *milieu* as Jane, the wartime *Daily Mirror* cartoon heroine, for whom things had gone seriously awry if she hadn't lost her clothes at the end of each escapade. Tabot is clearly fascinated by Joyce. She's exotic, blonde, ageless, unattached, flighty, venturesome, indomitably cheerful and generous, bronzed (we assume from Tabot's coy hints) all over. Her French is terrible, but she's got nice legs, so all is forgiven. Could Joyce represent Britain in Tabot's world-view?

In the latest episode of Tustabouïsse life, Joyce, who has integrated herself into local life remarkably well, joins her neighbours Tabot, Baptiste, Le Tiénot and Adelaide to go off mushrooming one afternoon after a preparatory *pastis*. Ever fashion-conscious, even when fossicking about in the autumn undergrowth for *cèpes* and *chanterelles*, she turns up wearing shorts, T-shirt and red ankle boots. In her ignorance she goes for the prettiest mushrooms, takes umbrage when Tabot throws them out because they're poisonous and strikes out on her own.

Unsurprisingly, she gets lost and spends the night under a bush. There's consternation in Tustabouïsse. Tabot passes a sleepless night (engagingly expressed in French as *une nuit blanche*, a white night), gets up to resume his search at first light, and the story shifts into another plane when Tabot discovers her red boots shining in the dawn light and Joyce curled up asleep with a doe and its fawn.

Joyce is irrepressibly cheerful about her misadventures, and starts chattering in a kind of Franglais: 'Plenty good!' she says gratefully, showing her grasp of English isn't all that hot, certainly not as hot as the coffee and croissants Tabot has thoughtfully brought her. '*On va déjeuner together?*' Tabot leaps at her suggestion to share breakfast and one can't help feeling this is what he's been waiting for all along. However this dawn idyll is unfeelingly shattered by a couple of statutory lines reminding us of the dangers of alcohol, in view of the brief mention of *pastis* earlier, which we must learn to consume with moderation. End of story.

Or is it? Is there perhaps a sub-plot, a hidden agenda, here? Could this be shorthand for France rescuing an errant Britain, a Britain reluctant to toe the European Union line, a Britain returned to the fold, grateful for nourishment at the hand of a friendly neighbour? Wondering if any more precious drops of insight could be squeezed out of *Le Recoin du Tabot*, I looked up *tustabouïsse* in the Occitan dictionary. You never know. Writers often do invest names with a particular significance.

Well, well. Literally meaning 'wooden-head', *tustabouïsse* has come to mean 'pig-headed, blinkered, obstinate'. Surprised, I looked up *tabot*: 'A thickset, stupid person. A bumpkin, a hick.' So much for that little notion, then. I'm clearly *nul* in that sort of analysis. I would do better to stick to ads for hunting dogs.

Dinner With Caesar

Maybe you remember the Inch War? I didn't pay much attention to it at the time, in the late 60s, being young and slim. It was something to do with losing weight, or at least not putting it on, promoted by one of the crispbread companies.

At that time, too, my attention to that and many other things could well have been distracted by the even younger and slimmer Liz Inch, the dashing dark-eyed beauty who taught in the classroom across the corridor from me. Every now and again the headmaster would ask her how the Inch War was going, and then retire to his sanctum in chuckling good humour to savour his little joke.

Well, the news from the Inch War battlefront is that we're losing heavily. Heavily, but gloriously. We don't put up much of a fight any more. In fact, we're close to unconditional and joyful surrender.

There are skirmishes every day with good things to eat, but the latest pitched battle was on Mayday, a public holiday here on whatever day it falls, and too bad if it happens to be a Sunday. We were invited to dine with the Caesars, that's to say César and Annie Desjoyeaux. They have a pleasant house in St Pons, a town where the old stone-built houses cluster round the cathedral and the more recent houses, Caesar's Palace among them, spread up the sides of the sunny St Pons valleys and enjoy views over the town with its ochre-tiled roofs gradually merging into the surrounding countryside.

César offered a choice of *apéritif.* Whisky? Suze, a bitter gentian-based drink generally diluted with tonic water or blackcurrant cordial? *Porto,* much lighter here than the treacly after-dinner ports customary in the UK? Muscat? *Pastis?*

No wine, you notice. Not as an *apéritif.* With the meal, yes; it's indispensable. But on its own, practically never. I learnt this essential truth shortly after arriving in France, and I was very surprised: I'd assumed that the entire French nation quaffs *rouge* morning, noon and night. To most French people, drinking wine on its own – except, perhaps, the very best champagne – is a naïve Anglo-Saxon habit, a misconception of the whole *raison d'être* of wine, which is to form a glorious, indissoluble and eternally youthful partnership with good things to eat. It's like buying a car and only driving it in reverse, not realising there are forward gears.

Eric Benoist, an insurance agent who deliberately cultivated a passing likeness to Groucho Marx, taught me this. He and I, myself newly resident in France and green as *crème de menthe*, slipped into the Bar du Centre in Labastide once for mid-afternoon refreshment. The company, all men, looked up briefly through the Gauloise fug, murmured *bonjour* and returned to their papers, cards or racing on television. Some were drinking *pastis*, others beer in the measure school milk used to come in. A few had coffee, others Perrier water. I wondered why none of them was drinking wine.

M. Benoist raised a superb eyebrow, adjusted his glasses, smoothed his moustache, cleared his throat and settled his tie, so that I wondered how much lower his fidgets would take him before the oracle pronounced. 'Monsieur Campbell,' he said, 'imagine having a young, beautiful, intelligent and willing partner.' Gripping stuff, so far.

'Imagine the many, varied and wonderful pleasures you could share. *Eh bien*, drinking wine on its own is like knowing no greater pleasure with her than' – he paused dramatically, to sniff the rose at his buttonhole – 'than cycling together to the Post Office.'

Voilà! César said as we were called to table: *L'Ananas Rupestre!* Annie appeared from the kitchen with half-pineapples, scooped out and filled with a mayonnaise of egg, celery, sweetcorn and pieces of pineapple, topped with *crevettes*, those big prawns that experts pull apart with a deft twist and flick of the fingers and which we, then, made such a flaky, sticky mess of. I wondered if the Caesars had chosen this *entrée* as much as pun-fodder as something tasty for their guests: *l'ananas* means the pineapple and *Rupestre* is the area of St Pons they live in, so the two together mean pineapple in the local style. But *la nana*, which sounds virtually the same as *l'ananas*, means in colloquial French the girl, doll, bird, crumpet and if you want any more you should consult Section 373 of Roget's Thesaurus. What César said could refer either to the dish Annie brought in, or to herself, 'the girl from round here'. Clever.

César's wine manners were fascinating. He'd brought up from his cellar (actually the coolest, darkest part of his garage) a Burgundy, of which he buys a case or two every year from a travelling salesman. Red, of course: white is drunk relatively little, being reserved to accompany special dishes which weren't on Annie's menu. He poured a little into his own glass first, to check the temperature: this is vital, because it affects the taste. Too cold, there will be a hard, almost metallic edge to it; too warm, it can become thin and acid, leaving a vinegary aftertaste. Just right, a little below room temperature . . . and obviously César was satisfied that the full, rich flower of the wine had opened up, because he went round the table pouring some into each glass. He didn't fill our glasses: pouring too much would be as boorish and inconsiderate as giving too little. Instead he made certain that our glasses were kept, if we wanted, topped up to the half-way point. It's a good system: little is wasted, and it allows guests, especially children, to add water, a surprisingly common practice.

When we were ready our *entrée* plates were taken away, but we were asked to keep our cutlery, wiping off any lingering streaks of mayonnaise on our bread. Annie asked how we would like our main course, *magret de canard*, breast of duck, done. There's a four-point scale:

1. *Saignant*, which means bleeding, lightly cooked.
2. *A point*, just right, which is the favourite French degree of cooking, with the outside of the meat browned, leaving the inside *rosé*, pink, not far off *saignant*.
3. *Bien cuit*, well cooked, which to British tastes means rare. The outside of the meat will be well browned, but although very tender the inside will still be pink and bloody.

4. French cooks roll their eyes in horror at the blasphemy of the fourth
   degree, *semelle*, which literally means sole. Of your boot, that is.
   This degree is sometimes called *Pirelli*, from the supposed likeness
   of your piece of meat to a section of car tyre. I've had it refused in
   some restaurants on the grounds that practically charred meat is
   bad for your health. Others have said that the professional pride of
   the *chef de cuisine* won't allow him to ruin a perfectly good piece of
   meat.

Annie didn't offer us the last option, which I would have preferred,
so I asked for *bien, bien cuit* and hoped for the best. She'd prepared
four vegetables, which was generous, as usually two are considered
enough: a purée of broccoli (a brilliant, almost fluorescent green) and
carrot (ditto, orange), green beans and courgettes. No potato: for
bulk, there was plenty of bread. Annie had done her best for me. The
duck was tender and succulent, a joy to eat, and her sauce was a
complete triumph: she'd laced a rich brown sauce with a little cognac
and *porto*, and had topped it with sliced *cèpes* sautée'd in olive oil.
César's Burgundy accompanied it to perfection, God was in his heaven
and all was well with the world.

Cheese next, then dessert, coffee, and finally a *digestif*, something
to aid digestion and encourage a comfortable night untroubled with
tummy-rumblings, heartburn or unsweet dreams. César produced,
quite unexpectedly, a bottle of Lagavulin, an Island malt whisky,
and poured about a thimbleful for those that wanted it. I
considered suggesting a slightly more ample measure, at least for
those who could pronounce the name, but I thought better of it.
They'd been generous enough already, and there was more to come:
just before we left, César and Annie presented each of the lady
guests with a bouquet of lily of the valley, traditional on Mayday.
Apparently it's to ensure their favours for the year ahead. A bargain,
if you ask me.

Mayday . . . *M'aidez* (help me): another pun for César, but it was
too late to call for help. We'd just lost another battle in the Inch War.

You had to hand it to us, though: we were such good losers. But I may have to think about getting a bicycle. Apart from taking something off the waistline, I quite like that idea of cycling to the Post Office.

It's An Ill Wind

Hervé Sénégas came from a neighbouring village to help with an end-of-winter tidy-up, clearing out ditches, burning leaves, that sort of thing. While he was bundling mimosa thinnings into the back of his ancient Peugeot pickup, a fire engine roared up the lane, lights flashing, siren wailing.

For some reason he's got it in for the local fire brigade. '*Ces mecs-là,*' he said, 'those blokes, they've got it made. Money for jam. There's no fire. They invent them half the time, just to fill in their time-sheets. Or they deliberately start a fire at the rubbish dump and then report it to themselves. Always at lunch-time, you notice. Time-and-a-half then, you see. *Scandaleux.*'

I don't know what the source of Hervé's grudge was, any more than I can remember my answer: something non-committal, probably, like *zut alors!* or *ô punaise!* (This means, improbably, 'oh drawing-pin!' – but it's a euphemism for something much stronger.) I've always had a healthy respect for the fire brigade, on the grounds that the more healthily you respect them, the quicker they'll come when you need them. I can't remember what day it was that this happened, either, but it certainly wasn't that extraordinary day not long before when we looked up and discovered that an entire hillside on the other side of the valley was ablaze.

It was a grey, timeless winter day, with the rolling contours of our valley dressed in the browns and greys of chestnut woods, leafless cherry trees and whiskery unpruned vineyards, in the dark greens of patches of Corsican pines and evergreen oaks. On remote hillsides smoke from bonfires of vine clippings or fallen leaves twirled upwards and hung still. Bonfires are supposedly strictly controlled in the Midi. Our little section of it was tinder-dry after several winter months with practically no rain. Bonfires are forbidden in the summer months, and if you want to burn garden rubbish in winter you have to obtain an *autorisation d'écobuage* from your local Mairie.

Ecobuage is one of those unguessable words that sends you scurrying to the dictionary and then muttering *zut alors!* or *ô punaise!* because it's not there. You have to consult the major French encyclopedia, Larousse, to find it, and even then it doesn't seem to apply. According to Larousse, *un écobuage* is a charcoal burner's fire, turf-covered and flameless. Here in Olargues, though, it's taken to mean the right to have a bonfire on your land.

Our *autorisation d'écobuage*, the one Hervé could wave in front of any passing fire-engine, allows bonfires on certain numbered sections of the property from November to March. They won't authorise burning any later because the fire hazard is too great. Our *autorisation* is validated with the official Mairie rubber stamp, so if any firewatcher sees a column of smoke rising from *parcelles* 317 or 318, they know it's our officially approved bonfire and they don't need to send in the fire brigade. This sounds a wonderfully logical and efficient method of controlling burning until you realise that the land registration map is years out of date and firewatchers, scanning the horizon from remote hill-top towers, only operate in summer.

In less time than it took to write this the weather changed, a stiff south-westerly breeze sprang up and somebody busy at his *écobuage* in the hamlet of La Mazarié on the hillside across the valley was in trouble. A few wind-borne sparks, a burning chestnut leaf, and in no time the brushwood, dead bracken and heather on the edge of the hamlet was ablaze, sweeping onwards before the wind and widening its path all the time. What had been a gentle plume of smoke at 2 pm was a roaring inferno by 5, devouring the woods, scrub and forestry plantations in its path and leaving a blackened, smoking waste behind it.

We looked across the valley horrified and fascinated. The whole hill was alight. Vast clouds of smoke swirled and gathered in the folds and gullies of the mountains above. Surely someone must have dialled 18 for the fire brigade? While we wondered, a helicopter overflew the blazing heath and woodland, appearing and disappearing in the smoke.

Presently flashing blue lights appeared on the main road which runs along the valley, and fire appliances began to toil up the hairpin-bended road to the Col de Fontfroide, a stiff climb that takes you up to 900 metres in 6 or 7 kilometres. Then there came the heavy drone of aircraft, distant at first, growing louder as they flew over the hills skirting the valley to the south and made for the smoke: the Canadairs had arrived.

The Canadairs are the élite of the fire-fighting force in an area particularly liable to forest fires. They're aircraft designed to carry several tons of water, and piloting them demands a particularly exacting training, as much for spot-on visual navigation as for consummate control when the aircraft suddenly bucks and rears once its load has been dropped, like a giant phoenix arising from the flames. They're equipped with scoops which enable them to refill their fuselage tanks flying low over the sea, or, as far inland as we are, over the lakes in the area.

Watching them in action is fascinating. They work in teams, pairs usually, doing their best to release their giant plumes of water along the line of the fire and just ahead of it, an operation needing great handling skill on account of the often very up-and-down terrain and the unfavourable wind direction. Legends grow up round the Canadairs, about ground fire-fighting crews enjoying the grilled sardines they find lying about the charred ground or – an old chestnut that surfaces every year – about the man unexpectedly scooped up with his Li-lo from a hitherto peaceful mid-lake zizz and dumped, the

Li-lo breaking his fall, amid the smoke and flames of a forest fire.

Night fell, and the Canadairs returned to their base, prevented by the darkness from completing their task, while the whole hill glowed with the embers. At the fire's edge immense flames still leaped and bounded like solar coronas. We went out to dinner with friends: when we returned after midnight it was burning as fiercely as ever.

Dinner-table reaction to our graphic descriptions didn't really rise above the *zut alors!* or *ô punaise!* level. Nor was *Midi Libre* enormously concerned. Fires are an all-too-frequent occurrence for any but the most catastrophic to make headline news. A tiny paragraph next day reported that someone's *écobuage* had got out of control. No property was threatened, no one had needed to be evacuated. Firemen in strength were keeping a 24-hour watch on the situation. The fire would burn itself out. Rain was forecast, anyway.

I didn't raise the subject with Hervé. He would have had something scathing to say about it. Who knows? Perhaps he was the man with the Li-lo.

OLARGUES

Bread And Circumstances

The St Pons goalkeeper, unbelievably, fielded a long, looping ball lazily drifted up towards him more in hope than anger, cradled it in his arms and stepped back over his goal-line, thus unwittingly giving away one of the easiest goals ever seen by the 30-odd spectators choosing to spend a Sunday afternoon watching the local St Pons – Olargues derby.

The referee, a solid, rock-like man endowed with stability rather than speed, ran the game more or less rooted to the centre spot and saw nothing of this. Realising from the hooting and bawling on the terraces behind the St Pons goal that something unusual had happened, he resolved the matter in an equally bizarre way: he banished the Olargues team into their own half, summoned the St Pons goalkeeper and one of the St Pons defenders to the penalty spot, bounced the ball between them and told them to get on with the game. No goal.

You might have expected a minor riot at this daylight robbery, but there was surprisingly little outcry from the Olargues team: no impassioned Latins mobbing the referee with wagging fingers, beating breasts and beseeching Maradona-like divine intervention. They probably hadn't noticed what had happened, to tell the truth, and anyway at that stage they were leading by two goals, went on to win 3-0, and afterwards the singing from their HQ, the Café Laissac, echoed long into the evening, in striking contrast with the glum faces in the St Pons HQ, the Bar du Palais.

I couldn't put a name at the time to The Man in Black, for the sound reason that he's usually more recognisable as The Man in White, M. Gosset the floury-handed master baker, who occasionally offers you an elbow to shake instead of a dough-stuck hand in his tiny Olargues *boulangerie*. A fine advertisement for his wares, M. Gosset is a Falstaffian figure with a mighty laugh, *embonpoint* to match, and a baker's sinewy biceps from much kneading. He also plays the clarinet: at least, if ever we fall to talking about music, he says he keeps meaning to get it out and give it a blow.

I'd enjoyed the match, I told him a few days later when I called in to buy one of his excellent *pains de campagne*, wholemeal loaves, which have ousted *baguettes* or *flûtes* as our daily bread. I asked him how the Olargues team had got on in their latest match, away to Le Poujol sur Orb, a village a few kilometres down the valley.

Eh bien, ils ont perdu, he said glumly. Well, they lost. *Mais je n'étais pas l'arbitre, figurez-vous*. But I wasn't the referee, you see. Was there a suspicion of a grin beginning to form along the lines of his flour-speckled beard?

Standing on the terraces, chin buried in winter coat, hands sunk deep in pockets, stamping feet against the cold – these aren't normally the images that spring to mind when you think of the Midi. 'Terraces' is misleading, too, because there aren't any: the best place to watch is from the raised lane which passes by the football ground on its way to the cypress-studded cemetery. Here spectators gather, scuffing their toes against the kerb, enjoying the panorama: the backdrop of Mt Caroux (you pronounce the x), ridged and cragged like a petrified dinosaur, framing the disused railway bridge, the vineyards, the orchards of cherry trees and olive groves in neat rows and, at their feet, the pitch and the goal area where visiting goalies make such interesting mistakes.

I haven't quite got the nerve – yet – to shout out instructions or imprecations in football-crowd French, and at this stage of following the fortunes of Olargues FC it's just as rewarding to recognise players out of their usual contexts. The gifted *ils-ne-passeront-pas* Olargues sweeper, for instance, is Olivier Fournier, the lad who does odd jobs for us on Saturday mornings. The luckless St Pons trainer I recognise as the man who drives the fork-lift truck at Bigmat, the St Pons builders' merchants, and his assistant is Gilles Guiraud, the St Pons florist. I suppose it's debatable what influences one's professional activity bring to the sports field, or vice versa: but M. Gosset's unflinching magistracy on the football field must owe something to his experience in the Olargues Bread War.

* * *

Olargues is a village of about 500 bread-eating souls, and their soul-food is catered for by two rival *boulangeries* lying in the heart of the village at each end of the rue Neuve. They're not easy to find unless you know your way about, and indeed the opening shots of the Bread War were fired by Gosset Granier, a father, mother and daughter team, putting up arrowed signs all over the village.

The other *boulangerie*, named Vivien et Rebecca after the young couple who run it, parried this with less sophisticated signs, in keeping with their rougher, grainier and crustier breads, compared with M. Gosset's fuller, smoother, doughier offerings.

But Vivien has a secret weapon, one that ensures that half Olargues, at any rate, follows the well-trodden path to his counter every day, because his Rebecca is unquestionably the prettiest woman in the village, with a beautiful figure owing only a little to the *pâtisseries* behind the counter: a vision of loveliness that sets the men of Olargues up for the day at least as much as their daily bread does. I suspect that many an elbow-clamped *flûte* reaches home ostensibly from Gosset Granier but actually having been wrapped by Rebecca's fair hand.

So the antes are constantly being upped. Window boxes of petunias and African marigolds appear outside Gosset Granier, so Rebecca's door is at once graced with geraniums in pots. The doorbell at Gosset Granier is suppressed in favour of a stuffed marmot which emits electronic wolf-whistles to welcome customers, and they follow this up with a slicing machine, never before seen in Olargues, where people tear at their bread as soon as cut it: a clanking, whirring second-hand Belgian juggernaut that scatters crumbs and flour far and wide. An A-board appears outside Vivien et Rebecca, announcing customer parking: maybe a hollow gesture in a village where the streets are mostly too narrow for cars.

But the latest attention-drawer is the new Gosset Granier cat, Zapi. Knots of people gather to watch it swinging in the variegated ivy trailing from the first floor window box. Word goes round Olargues that Zapi is *un numéro, un phénomène*. I went in to collect a *tarte aux myrtilles*, one of those mouth-watering confections from the *pâtissière* hands of Myriam, the Gossets' daughter, on one of our few wet days. Zapi darted in from from the bake-house, wrestled for a moment with the tip of my umbrella, skipped away and lay in an almost empty tray of croissants.

'He doesn't know what to do with himself,' Mme Gosset said, a comfortable, smiling woman. 'I don't like to put him out: the last time he got into Dr Bassi's car and went on his rounds with him.'

Dr Bassi is a local councillor, and cats or no cats hitching rides in his car, is anxious with the rest of the council to prevent the Olargues Bread War breaking out into open conflict. Healthy competition is one thing, bankruptcy, closure and distress is quite another. Wherever possible contracts for the supply of bread are distributed alternately, week or fortnight about, so Gosset Granier supplies the school *cantine* for the first fortnight in the month, while Vivian et Rebecca supply the *Maison de Retraite*, the Old Peoples' Home, and so on. They change over at half time. A smart piece of refereeing, worthy of M. Gosset himself.

* * *

The invitation was nothing very fancy, no stiff card – called 'Bristol' here – with gold edges, but just a folded card with a polite request to be present at the Mairie: Jean-Marc and Roselyne Gosset and their daughter Myriam would be honoured if we would arrive at 18h00.

Even after living several years in the Languedoc I still have a pathetic difficulty with the 24-hour clock. I learnt to be scrupulously careful when Mme Bounhol, a literal-minded St Pons soprano, once asked me when a particular rehearsal was to be. *A huit heures*, I replied, at 8 o'clock, meaning in the evening. I haven't forgotten the reproach in her eyes when she told me she'd found herself alone on the rehearsal room doorstep a couple of mornings later, and in rushing to get M. Bounhol off to work she hadn't had any breakfast.

So, to put it in upper infants arithmetic terms, 18 take away 12 equals 6, and at 6 o'clock we arrived at the Mairie and found a few of the village worthies already there, but not many: *le petit quart d'heure méditerranéen*, the little Mediterranean quarter of an hour – which means that you can turn up to almost any event at least 15 minutes late to find it hasn't started yet and that you aren't late after all – is too deeply rooted in the local psyche for 6 o'clock actually to mean 6 o'clock. By 6.20 maybe half the village was there, and things were ready to start. The other half was presumably the Vivian et Rebecca clientèle.

The reason for this *bringue*, to use one of Emilie's Bs, the one meaning a bunfight, was to celebrate a substantial honour that had come M. Gosset's way. The Hérault *département* has a chamber of commerce which awards prizes now and again for outstanding contributions to the quality of regional life, and the food categories include all the wonderful things that make this region such a gourmet's delight, sausage, jams, pâtés, dressings, nougat . . . and, of course, breads. First prize, and a trophy to match, had been awarded to Gosset Granier for their *pain de campagne*, their wholemeal loaf. A great honour, richly deserved. Mme Gosset – M. Gosset could hardly leave his ovens – had been the previous day to Montpellier to receive the trophy.

But Montpellier was remote, a 90-minute drive away. Clearly the trophy had to be re-presented in Olargues, in the presence of those without whom there would have been no trophy. The *maire*, seldom reluctant to expose his village to the limelight, would hand it over.

M. Gosset had baked a splendid celebratory *pain de campagne*, some 6 metres long, so long that it stretched along one wall of the Mairie reception hall, turned left and carried on, meticulously sliced in the Belgian slicing machine and surrounded, like a Blue Riband winner entering Long Island Sound, by lesser viands, pâtés, cheeses, salads, tomatoes, gherkins and slices of sausage. But where was the *maire*?

By 6.50 even the most hardened latecomers were shuffling about, looking at their watches, wondering where the *maire* was and how long it was going to be before this substantial spread could be attacked: there was a serious risk, in the summer heat, of the ice for the *pastis* melting. Elderly ladies fanned themselves, little children ran about. Lapdogs whimpered and scratched. A few excused themselves and left. I drifted off into a kind of philosophical reverie about the comparative durability of female beauty and Belgian slicing machines until my neighbour, M. Menielle, began to tell me his life story. It was worth hearing, a chastening *et-in-Arcadia-ego* reminder that there's always a price to pay for the leisure to dream in the Olargues sun of fair women and a full stomach, and that others have maybe chipped in on your behalf.

Daniel Menielle, a retired engineer, lives up the lane from us. Like many people who retire to the Languedoc, he comes from the north, from Le Havre. He's an active octogenarian who freewheels down to the village every morning for his *pain de campagne* with his spaniel Kuki trotting in front of him, and then puffing back up the incline, dismounting just by our fig tree and pushing the rest of the way.

When he was twenty, in the early years of World War 2, he was press-ganged into the STO, which stood for *Service de Travail Obligatoire*, the Compulsory Labour Service. This was a system of semi-slavery introduced by the Nazi occupying forces, and dodging this detested draft swelled the numbers joining the Resistance enormously. However, Daniel managed to escape, and made his way south through France with a price on his head, slipped over the Pyrenees into Spain where he was arrested, imprisoned and released without trial or explanation. He reached Morocco, headed for the nearest military base in what was then French North Africa, and enlisted with the Free French. He felt the proudest moment of his life when he set foot back on French soil in Operation Anvil, the southern French parallel to the Normandy landings, in August 1944 under the splendidly-named General de Lattre de Tassigny. As time rolls by there are fewer and fewer people left to tell this sort of stirring tale of patience, courage and determination.

And as time rolled by in the Mairie M. Gosset took it by the forelock, called for silence, said he for one wasn't going to wait any longer and that he proposed to make his speech of acceptance then and there and, if necessary, present himself with the trophy. The *maire* arrived in the middle, just as Rabelaisian laughter at M. Gosset's joke was dying away. It was the sort of joke that makes you really glad you worked so hard at *je suis, tu es, il est* in school or evening class and that your French is up to snuff. What's the difference between spermatozoa and the council workforce? Answer: None. One does all the work and the rest just swan about.

H'm.

So the *maire* presented a trophy already covered with Gosset fingerprints, half the village tucked in, and in the *mêlée* round the buffet, always anxious to draw musicians into the fold, I questioned M. Gosset a little more closely about his clarinet. *Ah, ça alors?* he said. Ah, that? He didn't know about that. He was a bit rusty. The truth was, he hadn't taken it out of its case since 1954. He's clearly used to long waits.

Pulling The Stops Out

It's a privilege to live in Olargues, one of France's prettiest villages. You're reminded of it every time you drive into the village: there's a sign at the side of the road saying *L'un des plus beaux villages de France*. It's official: there are only 142 other villages in France, a country with at least its fair share of pretty villages, enjoying the right to display this sign, *le label*, as it's called, and there are only two others in the Hérault *département*.

You can't just award yourself this accolade. *Le label* doesn't just drop out of the sky. You have to convince L'Association des Plus Beaux Villages de France that your village deserves it, and to become one of 143 selected from an entire nation of villages suggests that somebody has put a lot of effort into it one way or another.

It's true that Olargues gets off to a flying start. Most visitors are instantly seduced by the classic view of the village, the tumble of ancient stone-built and ochre-tiled houses spreading down the rocky wooded hillock topped with its elegant bell-tower, once part of a mediaeval *château*, and the Pont du Diable spanning the river Jaur, all set against the backdrop of Mt Caroux, the noble 1000m limestone *massif* which dominates the area. Scenically, then, it's seriously picturesque, and in fact a national competition called Paint Us Your Village, one of those country-wide community projects the French are so good at, first raised the possibility that Olargues might apply for the famous *L'un des plus beaux villages de France* accolade.

But scenic beauty isn't enough. The candidate village has to have several *sites classés*, Listed Buildings, Ancient Monuments and so on. Olargues has at least three: the hilltop bell-tower, which is the village's chief feature, the Pont du Diable and, as we shall see, the organ in the church.

But scenic beauty and a wealth of preservation-grade antiquity aren't enough either. There has to be clear evidence that the village is a thriving place with a vigorous community life. Provided these three criteria appear to have been met, the first visit by the inspectors of L'Association de Plus Beaux Villages de France is secret. If that goes well, a further delegation comes to make a final assessment, but overtly this time.

* * *

I knew nothing of all this when one summer morning the *maire* rang to ask if I could play the organ in a few days' time to a visiting delegation. He wasn't more specific. The Olargues organ is a gem, an organist's delight. However, knowing that it's a mid-19th-century single manual and pedal, tracker-action, Abbé Clergeau transposing system chamber organ, one of only six in France, might not turn you on to the same extent that it excited officials who classified it a Grade 1 Listed Instrument, thus making it one of the village's most precious attributes.

Playing this illustrious instrument for a visiting delegation was fraught with problems.

Problem 1: There was already an organist, the retired village postman.

Problem 2: The retired village postman, having worn out his legs in 40 years of delivering mail up and down the cobbled lanes and alleys of Olargues and the outlying hamlets, could no longer climb the steps to the organ loft without an enormous effort, and if ever he did manage to clamber up there it was unlikely that he would ever get down again.

Problem 3: Because the organ is a Listed Instrument, it falls under local government care, and the *curé* has no official say over who plays it and who doesn't.

Problem 4: The retired village postman's wife held the key to the church and so had the final word over who could be admitted into the church outside opening hours, so to speak, and who couldn't.

Problem 5: So scarce is building land in Olargues that the west wall of the church, where the organ is mounted, doubles as the east wall of the house next door. If the neighbours were of a nervous disposition, the Great Bass Trumpet on the organ might well sound as the Last Trump.

Not easy. It wasn't hard to understand why the Listed Instrument stayed mostly silent. It seemed that the retired postman was the key player in this Game of Tact and Diplomacy, so I went to see him. I found him kindly and helpful, anxious that the organ should be played and not moulder in idleness. With his co-operation the other problems, except possibly Problem 5, melted away.

On the eve of the appointed day, the *maire* called in person. Did I detect a worried man? The delegation was from the very top. On tomorrow's performance depended the award of *le label*. One of the other two *plus beaux* villages in the *département* had been found wanting and had had *le label* withdrawn. A shame and a disgrace to be avoided at all costs. Every Olargues *atout*, trump card, had to be played; all the stops had to be pulled out, so to speak. Further, we were expected at the official lunch afterwards in the Campotel.

He gave me the delegation's programme. There was to be a quick organ voluntary sandwiched between visits to the archaeological site (undertaken by volunteers from a European youth organisation called Concordia) round the hill-top bell-tower and the geology park by the riverside, where the labels (Devonian sandstone, pliocene conglomerate, that sort of thing) stood proudly but the rocks they identified hadn't actually arrived yet.

So I was rattling away up in the organ loft at Handel's *Arrival of the Queen of Sheba* (well, why not?) to an empty church when there came from below the unmistakeable sounds of a delegation from the very top. A nod to Josephine, who drew the Great Bass Trumpet stop, and I hoped the visitors felt like the President when trumpeters from the Garde Républicaine announce his entry. Was there any knocking on the wall from next door?

If there was, it was effectively muffled by the delegation of three climbing up to the organ loft, where the *maire* introduced me as *notre organiste presque titulaire*, our almost incumbent organist, as though the retired postman was on his last legs metaphorically as well as literally. We shook hands. One of the delegates asked if he could play, and a sneaking, un-musicianly feeling that he might be more capable than me – an easy possibility – was comfortably lulled when he tried a piece his mother had taught him when he was eight. Over and over again, he tried to get it right, while his fellow-delegates confirmed on their watches what their body clocks were telling them urgently: it was lunch-time.

At the Campotel everyone in Olargues who had ever taken any kind of initiative in the village for the public good had assembled. As in all *bringues* of this kind the courses kept coming and the wines to accompany them and nobody, not even the delegates on the top table, looked at their watches until well into a hazy sunlit afternoon. By then the *maire's* postprandial eulogy of the beauty and the heritage of his village, and of the exceptional talents and energy of the citizens he had the honour to administer, had become a pleasantly warm and drowsy memory.

They've planted pansies in the new beds round the *L'un des plus beaux villages de France* signs. Only annuals, it's true: you might have expected something longer-lasting to express confidence in the frequent renewal of *le label*. Recognition has come my way, too: after months of being introduced to this person and that as:

> *notre organiste <u>presque</u> titulaire*
>> or
>
> *notre organiste <u>quasiment</u> titulaire*
>> or
>
> *notre organiste <u>pratiquement</u> titulaire*

– a subtle graduation of French almost-but-not-quiteness, we were guests at the Mairie at an official reception for a visiting Russian choir. The *maire's* vote of thanks included a reference to *notre organiste titulaire*. No *presque*. No *quasiment*. No *pratiquement*. The complete *label,* as you might say.

They haven't planted pansies round me yet, nor round the retired postman: he's very much alive and . . . well, hardly kicking, but he's very relieved he won't have to climb the organ loft steps ever again.

Cover Design: The Digital Canvas Company
                   Forres
                   Scotland
                   bookcovers@digican.co.uk

Layout: Stephen M.L. Young
                   Elgin
                   Scotland
                   stephenmlyoung@aol.com

Font: Adobe Garamond (11pt)

Printed by   Imprimerie Périé
                   81230 Lacaune
                   France
                   imprimerie.perie@wanadoo.fr

Published by   ROMARIN
                   Flat 1, 66 Hencroft St South
                   SLOUGH
                   SL1 1RE
                   United Kingdom

                   (+44) (0)1753 674557

                   www.romarin.net